CHURCH,
EUCHARIST
AND PRIESTHOOD

CHURCH, EUCHARIST AND PRIESTHOOD

*A Theological Commentary on
"The Mystery and Worship
of the Most Holy Eucharist"*

Edward J. Kilmartin, S.J.

PAULIST PRESS
New York/Ramsey

Library of Congress
Catalog Card Number: 81-81343

ISBN: 0-8091-2386-X

Published by Paulist Press
545 Island Road, Ramsey, N.J. 07446

Printed and bound in the
United States of America

Contents

Preface

The title of this monograph expresses an important theme of modern Catholic theology. The rethinking of the relationship between Eucharist and Church has resulted in a new consciousness of the centrality of the Eucharist in the life of the Church. This is expressed in the slogan: The Eucharist makes the Church; the Church makes the Eucharist. This development has inevitably led to a clearer understanding of the relationship of the ordained and baptized both to the Eucharist and to the mission of the Church. Since "the Church makes the Eucharist," all the members have something in common. While roles are differentiated, both laity and ordained actively participate in the accomplishment of the Eucharistic celebration. Moreover the catchword "active participation of all in the Eucharist" brings to light a new appreciation of the nature and scope of the roles of the baptized and ordained in the mission of the Church. Since "the Eucharist makes the Church," manifests and realizes the Church, all who actively participate in the celebration are also those who are called on to participate in the mission of the Church to bring others under Christ, the head of the new people of God.

However the source of inspiration for the title is Pope John Paul II's Holy Thursday letter of 1980. The following pages contain a commentary on this letter in which the Pope, in his own way, offers a theological and pastoral reflection on the topic: Church, Eucharist and Priesthood.

The early completion of this commentary was made possible by the assistance of Mary Schaefer, a doctoral candidate in the field of liturgy at the University of Notre Dame.

I
Dominicae Cenae and
Modern Eucharistic Theology

Pope John Paul II's Holy Thursday letter of 1980, *Dominicae Cenae,* offers a sharp contrast to the numerous Vatican documents on the subject of Eucharistic doctrine and practice which have been issued with a view to the implementation of the Second Vatican Council's summons to liturgical renewal. Instead of the more official, impersonal style of communication, the Pope speaks in a very personal way, somewhat reminiscent of Pope John XXIII. He selects certain themes of Eucharistic theology and aspects of liturgical practice, accentuating what in his judgment should have special meaning for the modern Church. This way of treating the subject raises a question that is the particular concern of this monograph. To what extent does *Dominicae Cenae* reflect the overall approach of Vatican II to the mystery and cult of the Eucharist as well as the findings of modern liturgical studies and the newer Catholic theology?

The detailed commentary, based on the official Latin text, gives answers to various aspects of the question. A more general response is found in this introductory chapter. It is intended to provide the non-professional reader with the background needed for a more profitable reading of the commentary and the text (the Vatican English translation is found in the Appendix). The attempt is made to situate the theological reflection of *Dominicae Cenae* within the context of the method and findings of the newer Eucharistic theology which correspond to the fundamental lines of approach of Vatican II to the theme: Church, Eucharist and Ministerial Priesthood.

1. Theological Method of Dominicae Cenae

A correct evaluation of the theological strengths and weaknesses of *Dominicae Cenae* must take into account the fact that it is not simply a doctrinal treatise on the Eucharist. The declared intention of the Pope is to offer a personal witness of faith to the central mystery of the Eucharist with a view to securing, within the college of bishops, a common conviction and awareness of responsibility for the proper conduct of the liturgy of this mystery. The underlying pastoral concern is the fostering of reverence for the holy legacy of Jesus Christ. The basic message amounts to this: Only the attitude of profound reverence corresponds to the holiness of the mystery of the Eucharist.

Because of the intention, concern and message, the letter displays a multi-layered form of discourse. Frequent mention is made of the way in which the Eucharist should be celebrated, and the meaning of liturgical prescriptions related to the practical performance of the rite is recalled. Doctrinal statements, couched in the technical language of school theology, are introduced. But, at the same time, many concepts of scientific theology are used in the less precise sense which is characteristic of spiritual writings. Finally the Pope selects particular themes of Eucharistic theology. They correspond, in great part, to the ones which were judged by Vatican II to be especially relevant to the present situation of the Church: 1. the inseparable, reciprocal connection between Church and Eucharist which has profound consequences for the correct understanding of the nature of the local church and all pastoral ministry (4); 2. the Eucharistic liturgy as source of Christian ethical life and its missionary task (5, 6, 7); 3. the relationship of the ministerial priesthood and the common priesthood of all baptized to the Eucharist (2, 7, 8, 9, 12); 4. the theology and liturgy of the Word of God in relation to the Eucharist (2, 4, 10).

In spite of the wide range of topics, the general character of the letter as well as the expressed intention of the Pope (2.1) shows that he has no thought of presenting a systematic outline of Eucharistic theology. However he follows a theological method which is characteristic of one system. The reference to the danger of a partial, one-sided or erroneous use of the documents of Vatican II (12.8) implies the need to discern the fundamental lines and whole tendency of the conciliar decrees. This suggests that *Dominicae Cenae,* since it interprets the teaching of Vatican II, intends to follow the theological method espoused by the Council on the basis of its conception of salvation history.

Vatican II describes the Church as the people of God on the way to the promised land. This theme of pilgrimage brings out the concepts of point of departure, journey and goal. It highlights the founding event: the life, death and glorification of Christ together with the apostolic witness which has its primary expression in the New Testament; the historicity of the process by which the Gospel is handed on to each generation and responds to its new questions and problems; the blessed fulfillment yet to come. In the perspective of this understanding of salvation history, Vatican II's *Decree on the Training of Priests* speaks of the proper methodology of dogmatic theology (16).

The older dogmatic method began with the teaching of the magisterium: definitions of councils and other official doctrinal texts. Scripture and tradition were introduced to show how this teaching is found in revelation. There followed speculative clarification and integration of particular doctrines within the whole of revelation. In the *Decree on the Training of Priests* it is recommended that, first, the relevant scriptural themes be investigated and then tradition and the development of the truths of faith in history. Afterward the attempt should be made to situate these truths within the whole of revelation "with St. Thomas as master." Finally it is noted that these methodological steps should be undertaken with a view to seeking answers to modern problems "in the light of revelation, to apply its eternal truths to the changing conditions of human affairs and to express them in language which people of the modern world will understand."

The older method had the advantage of bringing to light important facts about the historical development of the life of faith. On the other hand, it tended to reduce Scripture to a storehouse of prooftexts for the dogmatic teaching of the magisterium. Hence it gave the impression that the temporally and historically conditioned dogmatic formulas are the timelessly valid and clearest expression of the truth of revelation under consideration.

The shift in methodology, recommended by Vatican II, originates in a new consciousness of the relationship between Scripture and tradition. Scripture is restored to its original normative place; the documents of tradition are seen and evaluated as part of the continuous process of interpretation in which the magisterium interprets the revelation of God in the Scriptures in completely determined historical situations of the life of faith.

Dogma, therefore, is considered relative in a twofold sense. It stands at the service of the original Word of God. At the same time it responds to questions of Christians in definite periods of history by showing how revelation should be understood in concrete situations. Dogmas stand under the authority of the Word of God in Scripture and, at the same time, show how believers should respond to this Word as they respond to questions peculiar to their cultural and historical context.

The title of the first section of *Dominicae Cenae* corresponds to the dogmatic method of Vatican II, but the development of the theme, "The Eucharistic Mystery in the Life of the Church and of the Priest," is carried out in the style of the pre-conciliar Scholastic theology. It begins with a discussion of "Eucharist and Priesthood." The pericope which treats "Eucharist and Church" (4) is abruptly inserted afterward and does not contain a development of the ecclesiological dimension of the hierarchical priesthood's Eucharistic service. In other words, the basic tendency of the *Dogmatic Constitution on the Church* of Vatican II does not serve as guide. This Constitution begins with "The People of God" (ch. II) and then takes up the question of the role of the ordained ministry within the Church under the title: "The Church Is Hierarchical" (ch. III).

The argument for the special relationship of the hierarchical priesthood to the Eucharist also is constructed along the lines of the older dogmatic method. Trent's *Decree on the Sacrifice of the Mass* provides the chief source. To support this teaching early liturgical texts are cited. Also two passages from Scripture are inserted which are only marginally relevant. Finally documents from Vatican II are introduced in a footnote to support a concluding explanation of the central place of the celebration of the Eucharist in the exercise of the hierarchical ministry (2.2).

In this instance *Dominicae Cenae* follows the example of Vatican II's *Dogmatic Constitution on the Church* which fails to develop the ecclesiological foundation of the hierarchical ministry of the Eucharist. Chapter II of this Constitution teaches that the Church is, in the first place, the whole body of the faithful united in Christ. In this context one might expect that the Eucharistic ministry of the hierarchy would be traced back to its ecclesiological basis. But the Constitution is not perfect. By way of compromise the special role of the hierarchy in the Eucharist is simply expressed in terms of the Tridentine concept of "power of consecration." Consequently the theological method clashes with that employed at the outset of Chapter II. Instead of approaching the subject from the viewpoint of biblical theology, an appeal is made to the teaching of the magisterium (10.2 and footnotes 2, 3).

2. Eucharist and Priesthood

Modern Catholic theology presents a different description of the origin of the ministerial priesthood from that of the Council of Trent and post-Tridentine theology. The Fathers of the Council of Trent were convinced that the sacrament of the priesthood was instituted at the Last Supper at the moment of the institution of the Eucharist and together with it. They interpreted the words "Do this in memory of me" to be a command of Jesus, ordering the apostles and their successors in the priesthood to celebrate the Eucharist. Modern dogmatic theology does not simply reject this teaching. Rather it reads it within the contemporary historical context of the sixteenth century and in relation to the whole of tradition.

The Council of Trent had to settle pressing problems in the wake of Reformation criticism of the offices of the Church. At the forefront of the debate were the questions of the jurisdictional power of the episcopacy and the presbyteral power of order which enables presbyters to consecrate the Eucharistic bread and wine and to absolve sinners. Because of the uncertainties concerning episcopal office, the Council was unable to formulate a satisfactory comprehensive theology of the episcopate. Hence it was also unable to offer an adequate theology of the presbyterate. In the latter case Trent settled for a strong affirmation of the sacramental function peculiar to this office. A narrow cultic view was projected which subsequently determined the starting point for a systematic presentation of the presbyterate within Catholic school theology.

Modern Catholic dogmatic theology, profiting from the advances in historical studies and biblical exegesis, is more nuanced and cautious in the description of the institution of the ministerial priesthood and its relation to the Eucharist. It begins with the New Testament witness since this has a fundamentally normative value for Christian faith and life. It then investigates the historical process of development of the theology and practice of the ministerial priesthood. On the basis of the modern historical and exegetical studies, especially in view of the biblical descriptions of office, it can make the following statements about the relationship of the Eucharist and ministerial priesthood in the early Church:

1. The requirement of the office of bishop or presbyter for the exercise of leadership of the Eucharist can neither be affirmed nor denied on the basis of the New Testament evidence.

2. Within the New Testament perspective the ministry of presbyter and bishop can be called priestly primarily because in all their Church related activities they mediate the priestly service of Jesus Christ. The qualification "priestly" cannot be reserved for their activity in the celebration of the Eucharist.

3. At the beginning of the second century the Eucharist was celebrated in communities of the united Church under the supervision of the bishop or another office bearer subordinate to him. This coincides with the conscious awareness of the central role of the Eucharistic celebration in the mediation of the saving word and action of the risen Lord.

Reflection on the events connected with the origin of the Church also requires of modern Catholic theology a presentation of the institution of the ministerial priesthood which differs from that of Trent. According to the New Testament both what Jesus said and did during his earthly life and also his death, resurrection and sending of the Spirit are constitutive elements for Church and sacraments. In the biblical view the Church is fully constituted when that condition is fulfilled which makes possible the abiding saving presence of God in the world. This condition is the death of Jesus and his glorification together with the mission of the Spirit. Consequently the Last Supper, before the death and resurrection and mission of the Spirit, is not in the strictly theological sense the first Eucharistic celebration of the apostolic Church. Also the offices of the Church are only fully constituted with the event of the death, resurrection and mission of the Spirit.

In contrast to this approach, *Dominicae Cenae* paraphrases the teaching of the Council of Trent about the institution of the sacrament of the priesthood in connection with the institution of the Eucharist. It does not allude to the difficulties underlying Trent's interpretation of the historical facts (2.2). Also the founding of the Church is described in terms of what the earthly Jesus said and did at the Last Supper. On that occasion the twelve apostles entered into sacramental communion with the Son of God and "from that moment" the Church "is being built up through the same communion with the Son of God. . . ." (4.1).

Especially noticeable throughout the letter is the lack of attention to the pneumatological dimension of the ministerial priesthood. Only once is the Spirit mentioned in this connection. The anointing of the hands of the priest, peculiar to the Western ordination rite, is interpreted as a gesture of impetration for the grace and power of the Spirit to be given to these hands (11.11). Moreover, drawing on the Tridentine theology of power of consecration, the letter speaks of the human priest as the acting subject of the consecration of the Eucharistic bread and wine (11.11) and of the "consecration by the priest" (9.7). While *Dominicae Cenae* frequently refers to the New Mass of Paul VI, in this instance it does not allude to what the new Eucharistic Prayers say about the Spirit as subject of the Eucharistic consecration.

The Tridentine conceptual horizon and the older dogmatic method, chosen by *Dominicae Cenae,* lead to incomplete statements about Eucharist and priesthood. However it would be a mistake to assume from the foregoing observations that the Pope has no more to say about the subject or that he remains bound by the narrow view of the Council of Trent. He clearly moves beyond the Tridentine definition of priest. Following the teaching of Vatican II, he does not reduce the comprehensive ministry of the Gospel bestowed in the ordination of the presbyter to an empowerment for the celebration of the Eucharist and other sacraments. Moreover, again in keeping with Vatican II's teaching, he develops certain aspects of the ecclesiological dimension of the Eucharist. *Dominicae Cenae* stresses that the active subject of the liturgy of the Eucharist is the whole Christ, head and members: the whole community united with Christ. This was something neglected by Trent.

3. Sacrificial Character of the Eucharist

Modern Eucharistic theology begins its reflection on the Eucharistic sacrifice with the New Testament concept of sacrifice and its description of the way in which the sacrificial devotion of Jesus is symbolically represented in the accounts of the institution of the Eucharist.

The New Testament uses the word "sacrifice" in a Christian context to describe the self-offering of Jesus and the Christian. Jesus' sacrifice consists in his self-offering to the Father on behalf of mankind. The sacrifice of Christians consists in the offering of self, in union with the offering of Christ, which includes like sentiments of love and obedience toward the Father also on behalf of mankind.

However the New Testament has something more to say about the self-offering of Jesus which is also applicable to the self-offering of Christians. The aspect of the initiative of the Father is important for the correct understanding of the mystery of the self-offering of Jesus. For the proper grounds of the offering of Jesus cannot be simply traced back to his initiative. Rather, in this regard, the New Testament turns upside down the history of religions' understanding of sacrifice. The movement is not, in the first place, from human beings to God. It is quite the opposite. This is implicitly expressed in the scriptural use of the passive voice to describe the delivery of Jesus into the hands of sinners: "This is my body which is given . . ." (Lk. 22:19); "On the night he was handed over . . ." (1 Cor. 11:23). The Fourth Gospel interprets this with the words: "For God so loved the world that he gave his only Son" (Jn. 3:16). In a similar way Paul refers to the God "who did not spare his own Son but gave him up for us all" (Rom 3:32). The author of 2 Corinthians identifies God as the one who "through Christ reconciled the world to himself . . . that is, God was in Christ reconciling the world to himself" (2 Cor. 5:18–19).

From the perspective of John, Paul and the Pauline tradition, the offering which the dying Jesus makes of himself is the expression of the Father's turning toward us. In other words, the love of God is the ultimate source of the self-offering of the Son to the Father on behalf of the world. To speak of the self-offering of Jesus on the cross means, for the eyes of faith, to perceive the movement of the offering of the Father himself to us, to accept it and give thanks for it. Correspondingly, to speak of the self-offering of the Christian on behalf of others includes, in the New Testament perspective, the movement of God to mankind through other human beings. God makes his entrance into the world as loving God through the self-offering of Christ and the self-offering of those who live in Christ.

This concept of sacrifice—self-offering of the Father, Christ and Christians—provides modern Eucharistic theology with a way of expressing the very core of the meaning of the Eucharist. It thematizes the loving communion between God and mankind which is expressed and realized in the Eucharist. But what is the essential liturgical expression of this sacrifice in the Eucharistic celebration?

According to the accounts of the institution of the Eucharist, the outward form of the representation of the sacrificial devotion of Jesus at the Last Supper is his self-offering in the signs of food. Christ's intention is to offer himself in such a way that he is simultaneously received, eaten. There exists, therefore, an intrinsic relation between the personal self-offering of Jesus, together with that of his body, the Church, and the Eucharistic sharing of food and drink which is its efficacious sign.

This perspective poses a problem for the newer Eucharistic theology. For it collides with the traditional identification of the consecration of the bread and wine with the "sacrificial act" of the Eucharist. Limiting the sacrificial act to the sacramental representation of the offering and immolation of the cross which takes place in the consecration of the bread and wine makes the meal aspect an appendage, even if it is called a "sacrificial meal." The conclusion is, therefore, drawn that the question of the sacrificial act of the priest at the "moment of consecration" must be embedded in the wider ecclesiological context of the body of Christ theology of St. Augustine.

From these considerations the following basic statements about the Eucharist as sacrifice of the Church emerge:

1. The sharing of the body and blood of Christ makes the participants into his body and draws them into his destiny. The Eucharistic Christ is personally present to change mankind into the true body of Christ and so to enable it to become an acceptable offering.

2. The Eucharistic Christ is present as the crucified Lord. Therefore the Eucharist is anchored in the death of the cross. But this does not signify that in the frequent celebrations of the Eucharist the once for all death of the cross is repeated. For in the passage from suffering to glory Jesus was established as the eternal High Priest. This makes his self-offering into a permanent being-for-us. In the Eucharist the death of the cross is re-presented, recalled and applied. In other words, the Eucharist is the sacramental symbolic form under which the eternally enduring self-offering of Christ to the Father on behalf of mankind obtains power over the participants in the Holy Spirit.

This understanding makes clear that the Church adds nothing to the sacrifice of the cross. It does not renew or repeat what happened once for all; it undertakes nothing on its own in the offering of the body and blood of Christ. Rather the Church is taken up into his self-offering. It is enabled to participate in this act in the power of the Spirit.

3. The role of the Holy Spirit is decisive in the realization of the presence of the sacrifice of the cross in the Mass. The presence of this sacrifice which includes the turning of the Father to us and the response of Jesus, accepting and affirming the movement of God the Father in love, happens in the power of the Spirit. It is precisely the action of the Spirit which grounds the sacramental quality of the Eucharist and together with the movement of the Father in the self-offering of the Son accounts for its holy character.

A more systematic outline of the newer Eucharistic theology takes the following form. Through the once for all self-offering of Jesus Christ, he has become eternal High Priest. In the action of the

Eucharist and the words which interpret it, his eternally efficacious self-offering for us is recalled and proclaimed. In the giving of the Eucharistic gifts as holy food, this self-offering is both represented and applied. Thus the Eucharist represents the reality of the cross in the form of a sacramental memorial meal.

In itself the Eucharistic celebration is not a sacrifice alongside or in addition to that of the cross. Rather it is the communication of the sacrifice of the cross to the community. The Eucharist can be called the sacrifice of the Church insofar as the Church shares the paschal event, lives in and from Christ. The Eucharist has the goal of realizing the offering of the whole Christ: head and members, the participation of the members in the self-offering of Christ.

The visible sign of the self-offering of Christ in the Eucharist and of the participants' insertion into this self-offering is the meal. It signifies on the one hand Jesus Christ's offering of himself as food and, on the other, the thankful acceptance of this giving of himself by the participants.

This self-offering includes also the turning of the Father to the participants in the Son and the movement of the Son of Man to the Father. The participants are summoned to insert themselves into both movements: in the direction of the turning of the Father toward humanity and in the movement of the Son to the Father. For the Eucharist calls the participants to serve the others and, at the same time, to hope and trust in the Father as did the Son.

The role of the Father in the self-offering of the Son and the work of the Spirit in rendering present this saving act are the proper grounds for the sacred character of the Mass, its cultic-sacramental quality.

As in the case of the newer Eucharistic theology, *Dominicae Cenae* employs the concept of sacrifice as a focal point for its reflection. The Eucharist is "above all a sacrifice" (9.1). But the point of departure for the development of this theme is the way of speaking and thinking of the Council of Trent and post-Tridentine theology. As a result it does not transcend certain difficulties inherent in that theological exposition.

The late medieval and Renaissance Scholastic theology did not work out a differentiated way of speaking about the liturgical-ceremonial aspects and the theology of the Mass. Hence the Council of

Trent was not equipped to give a clear answer to the practical griev- ances of the Reformers which often contained a wrong or false con- cept of the Mass itself. The intermingling of practice, rites and theology in the charges of the Reformers made it difficult for Trent to speak in a coherent way about the Eucharistic sacrifice as it at- tempted to respond.

In the *Decree on the Mass* the New Testament sayings about the self-offering of Christ are mixed up with a ritual concept of sacrifice derived from Old Testament animal and food offerings. Thus in Chapter I of the *doctrina* Christ is said to have given his body and blood to the apostles "in order that they offer them." This is an ob- vious reference to the liturgical level of the outward sign. But in Chapter II of the same *doctrina* a different meaning is given to the word "offer." Here the New Testament concept of sacrifice—self-of- fering—comes into play with reference to Christ's offering of himself on the cross and in the Mass.

This intertwining of the ritual and dogmatic ways of speaking or even an unreflective identification of the history of religions' con- cept of sacrifice (victim distinguished from priest) with the New Tes- tament concept (identification of priest and victim) led to continued difficulties and misunderstandings. In the post-Tridentine theology it resulted in a presentation of the Eucharistic sacrifice along the lines of the Old Testament model which the Epistle to the Hebrews rejects as passé. For the act of offering to God is simply placed on the level of the outward sign of the liturgical action. As a result Catholic theo- logians could speak of a kind of repetition or renewal of the sacrifice of the cross in the Mass.

The way of speaking and thinking of Trent is reflected in *Do- minicae Cenae.* In accord with Trent, the letter speaks of the Savior as both priest and victim of the Eucharistic sacrifice. On the other hand the human priest is said to perform "a sacrificial act," in virtue of the power received in ordination, "which refers mankind to God" (9.1–2). This second statement must refer to the liturgical "offering." But the mode of expression collides with that of Hebrews 10:14 as well as with the statement of the Pope concerning Christ as "author and principal subject" of the Eucharistic sacrifice (8.4).

Dominicae Cenae also accepts the Tridentine separation of the Mass as sacrificial action from the Eucharist as sacrificial meal. The consecration by the priest is the "sacrificial act." In 9.6 it is stated that those who participate in the Eucharist with faith are conscious that it is a "sacrifice, i.e., consecrated oblation. For the bread and wine exhibited on the altar . . . are consecrated to become . . . the body given and the blood shed by Christ himself." Thus *Dominicae Cenae* neglects to include the "sacrificial act" in the wider ecclesiological context which comes to light through the more penetrating understanding of the relation between sacrifice and meal.

In the presentation of the relationship of the sacrifice of the cross to the Eucharist, *Dominicae Cenae* follows the main lines of the Tridentine teaching. It affirms that Christ celebrated sacramentally the mystery of the passion at the Last Supper (8.3). But only with reference to the Eucharist is it stated that "because of the consecration the species of bread and wine represent in a sacramental and unbloody way the bloody propitiatory sacrifice which he offered to the Father on the cross. . . ." (9.6). Hence just as the Council of Trent did, the Pope attributes a sacrificial character to the Last Supper but applies the notion of "propitiatory sacrifice" only to the Eucharist. The Mass alone, for Trent and the Pope, represents, recalls and applies the propitiatory sacrifice of the cross.

However in the paragraph of *Dominicae Cenae* which follows 9.6, a terminological breakdown occurs. The sacrifice of the cross is said to be "renewed (*renovatur*) in a sacramental way on the altar" (9.7). The language of the post-Tridentine theology is substituted for that of Trent. However this does not mean that the Pope favors the kind of theory of the sacrifice of the Mass associated with the language of "renewal." The meaning of *renovare* should be identified with Trent's *repraesentare*. Otherwise it collides with the concept of the sacramental representation of the sacrifice of the cross in the Eucharist which the Pope has just affirmed. Trent itself, as well as Vatican II, never uses *renovare* in this context. Its use in *Dominicae Cenae* should perhaps be attributed to early theological training.

The argument for the holy character of the Mass is also developed within the Tridentine outlook. At the Last Supper Christ instituted a "holy rite, the primary constitutive liturgy" (8.3). The Mass, therefore, is holy because it contains the action of Christ in the form of this rite. However, the holy character of the Mass cannot be simply grounded on this christomonistic explanation: on what Christ did at the Last Supper and does in the Mass. The Trinitarian basis must be introduced: the initiative of God the Father in the self-offering of the Son and the work of the Holy Spirit. In this latter connection it is noteworthy that the Holy Spirit plays no constitutive role in the description of the Eucharistic event. Both in the arguments for the grounding of the holiness of the Eucharist and its sacramental character the pneumatological dimension is lacking.

Conclusion

On the whole, *Dominicae Cenae* takes up the Catholic position on the Eucharist from the standpoint of the Tridentine problematic. The gains of the newer Eucharistic theology are only partially taken into account. Also the important ecumenical statements on the ministerial priesthood and the Eucharist, developed over the last fifteen years, are ignored. An opening toward the Eastern Orthodox Churches may be indicated in the frequent references to that tradition. But at the same time references to their theology of the Spirit are omitted.

The Pope is above all concerned with deepening the unity of the Catholic Church and with resolving tensions which exist in the Church due to the post-conciliar liturgical renewal. Hence the choice of subjects is influenced by the objections of reactionary groups to the changes in the liturgy. The mode of argumentation is also probably determined in great part by the desire to speak to "Tridentine" Catholics within their frame of reference.

In view of the complex literary genre of the letter it is perhaps too much to expect it to measure up to the criticism of scientific theology. The neglect of the newer Eucharistic theology should not, however, be taken as a rejection. One does justice to *Dominicae Cenae* if it is read on its own terms. It is a personal witness of faith of a pastoral Pope who in his own way seeks to call attention to the holy legacy of Jesus Christ and so to the responsibility which all Christians have toward it. It can, therefore, be read as a word of encouragement to theologians to take seriously their task of presenting correct doctrine of the Eucharist.

II
Commentary on the
Holy Thursday Letter
of Pope John Paul II:
Dominicae Cenae

On the First Sunday of Lent, February 24, 1980, Pope John Paul II addressed a letter to all the bishops in communion with Rome on the subject of "the mystery and cult of the Most Holy Eucharist."[1] The introduction explains that the letter is intended for Holy Thursday, "the annual feast of priests." It is a sequel to the one of April 8, 1979, written for the same occasion, which reaffirmed the Vatican position on clerical celibacy.[2]

Dominicae Cenae falls into the class of *epistulae,* circular letters sent to the whole episcopal college.[3] Nevertheless priests and deacons are singled out as special addressees since the Pope deals with "certain aspects of the Eucharistic mystery and its impact on the lives of those who are ministers of it." In addition, the contents of this document indicate that a much wider audience is also envisioned in a special way. The unusually large number of Eastern Church sources, particularly liturgical texts, merits attention. By showing that these sources display the same understanding of the Eucharist as that of the ancient and modern Catholic Church, the Pope contributes to the work of the recently established international Orthodox-Roman Catholic dialogue which has chosen for study the sacraments and, in particular, points of contact between the two churches in Eucharistic faith and practice.[4] But the chief reason for employing the witness of the Eastern tradition lies elsewhere. It serves as one way of assuring those Roman Catholics, disturbed or alienated by the post-Vatican II liturgical "renewal,"[5] that the Catholic Church remains faithful to the liturgical tradition of the undivided Church of the first millennium.

Dominicae Cenae must be considered one of the more significant papal contributions to the theology of the Eucharist in the twentieth century. Worthy of the attention not only of pastors and laity but also of scholars who specialize in the areas of liturgy, theology and spirituality of the Eucharist, it contains three main sections with thirteen chapters. A fundamental statement about the relation of the priest to the Eucharist is followed by a discussion of the holy and sacrificial character of this mystery. The last section treats the Liturgy of the Word and Holy Communion. This plan calls for some comment. But first the use of the phrase "annual feast of priests" merits consideration.

Feast of Priestly People or Feast of Priests. The early medieval Roman episcopal liturgy of Holy Thursday was a preparation for the paschal celebration. The characteristic trait was reconciliation of penitents and, eventually, the blessing of oils for the rite of initiation. The Eucharist, originally linked with Easter before the Jerusalem innovations of the fourth century, had a place in this liturgy as a nonfestal Mass. But under the impetus of medieval piety it came more and more to the foreground in the chrism Mass of Holy Thursday. Urban IV provides one witness to this in the bull *Transiturus* (1264) which inaugurated the feast of *Corpus Christi:* "On the day of the Supper of the Lord when Christ himself instituted this sacrament, the universal Church, occupied with the reconciliation of sinners, the confection of the holy chrism, the fulfilling of the command to wash the feet and other things, cannot be without the celebration of this sacrament, the greatest of all."[6]

The sixteenth century Council of Trent, following the more common teaching of Scholastic theology, affirmed that the sacrament of the priesthood originated at the Last Supper. But this did not have immediate repercussions on the liturgy of Holy Thursday. The movement toward the formulation of an explicit liturgical reference to the relationship of the ministerial priesthood and Holy

Thursday first received official encouragement in the *Ordo hebdomadae sanctae* of 1955. In the General Reform of Holy Week it is suggested that one of the themes of the evening Mass of Holy Thursday be the institution of the *ordo sacerdotalis*. A further development occurred when Paul VI made public, on February 10, 1970, two new changes in the provisional revision of the chrism Mass of 1965. A new preface was added which refers to the priesthood of Christ, the royal priesthood of the people and the ministry of priests. In addition a form of renewal of priestly promises was inserted. Other changes are also found in the chrism Mass of the *Missale Romanum* of Paul VI, promulgated on March 26, 1970, which point in the direction of the explicit intention to clericalize this liturgy. For example, the opening collect does not refer to the whole congregation. Setting aside the rules of the venerable Roman liturgical tradition, this prayer is made on behalf of "us" who have been given "a share in his (=Christ's) consecration to priestly service in your Church."[7]

These changes in the chrism Mass correspond to what, in fact, it had become in the course of time: a clerical affair traditionally celebrated without a significant number of cathedral parishioners, to say nothing of members of other parishes of the diocese. But they hardly coincide with the original intention behind the renewal of the chrism Mass: to make it a celebration of the episcopal local church in its entirety as a priestly people. For this reason the reaction of liturgists has been, on the whole, rather cool toward the shifting of emphasis to one segment of the local church in the solemn liturgy of the day, and especially to the more general description of Holy Thursday as the "annual feast of priests."[8]

Sources of the Plan and Content. The second preliminary remark concerns the source or sources which influenced the plan of the letter. The division reflects the traditional Scholastic christomonistic approach to the theology of the Eucharist which neglects the pneumatological dimension. It also follows fairly closely the typical systematic development of the post-Tridentine Scholastic theologies: real presence, Communion and sacrifice. However, the theology of *Dominicae Cenae* transcends the typical Scholastic synthesis which was unable to adequately express the inner relation between the sacrament of the body and blood of Christ and the sacrifice of the Mass.

In line with twentieth century Catholic Eucharistic theology, the letter formulates the relationship of dependence in terms of *sacramental sacrifice* and *sacrificial sacrament.*[9] This subject is discussed in the commentary on Section II of *Dominicae Cenae.* For now it suffices to note that the sacrificial theme provides the context for understanding the rest of the Eucharistic theology of the letter. However it is only understandable in light of what is said in Section I.

While Catholic theology had a role to play in the plan of the letter, there is evidence that the development and content were influenced more by the pastoral concern to cope with various objections raised by traditionalist Catholics to the theology of the Eucharist found in the New Mass of Paul VI and the liturgical changes initiated by it.[10] For example, it can be shown that the "certain aspects" of Eucharistic theology and practice selected for comment correspond to the various criticisms leveled against the New Mass by Bishop Marcel Lefebvre.[11]

Section I
The Eucharistic Mystery in the Life
of the Church and of the Priest.

This section includes two groups of themes which roughly correspond to what may be termed the vertical and horizontal dimensions of the Eucharist. These are: (1) the Eucharistic basis of the priesthood and Church and the special character of Eucharistic cult; (2) the connection between the Eucharist and charity, neighbor and life. The vertical dimension, from which the horizontal derives, is understood to be the bond which links the ministerial priesthood to the common priesthood of the baptized.

Ch. 2: Eucharist and Priesthood.

The intimate link between the ministerial priesthood and the Eucharist is affirmed by distinguishing the relationship of the ordained ministries (bishop, priest, deacon) to the two parts of the Mass. These ministries "normally begin with the proclamation of the Gospel,"[12] but "are in closest connection with the Eucharist." The relation between the institution of the Eucharist and the institution of the "sacrament of the priesthood" shows that the "principal and central *raison d'être* of the priesthood is the Eucharist." Here *Dominicae Cenae* echoes the teaching of the Council of Trent. It states that the ministerial priesthood "arose simultaneously with the institution of the Eucharist and together with it." This corresponds to the text of Trent to which reference is made: ". . . by the words 'Do this in memory of me' (Lk. 22:19; 1 Cor. 11:24), Christ . . . instituted (*instituisse*) the apostles priests and directed that they and other priests offer his body and blood."[13]

The Reception of the Council of Trent, Session xxii, Canon 2, by Dominicae Cenae. This canon of Trent presupposes that when the apostles were received into the *ordo sacerdotalis* they obtained the *potestas sacra* to consecrate the bread and wine and to offer the sacramental body and blood of Christ to the Father. But it also takes for granted that the apostles were only fully constituted in their mission and so received the power to forgive sins and rule after the resurrection, when Christ bestowed on them the Holy Spirit (Jn. 20:22ff.).[14]

The theology of the *ordo sacerdotalis* accepted by the majority at Trent held that the highest degree was the presbyterate. A minority at Trent followed the school of Salamanca which maintained that the episcopate was the highest instance of this *ordo* and that episcopal ordination itself conferred both the power over the sacraments and the power of jurisdiction (teaching and governing). But all agreed that the priesthood received by the apostles at the Last Supper corresponds to that of the presbyterate and that this *ordo* does not include a *potestas sacra,* received in ordination, which pertains to the sphere of jurisdiction.[15] On the other hand, Vatican II—which does not take up the precise question posed at Trent concerning the relation of the institution of the Eucharist to the priesthood of the apostles—clearly states that the *potestas sacra,* received in episcopal ordination, includes the aspects of power of order and jurisdiction. It likewise speaks in an analogous way of the *potestas sacra* received in presbyteral ordination.[16]

Dominicae Cenae accepts the teaching of Trent on the relation between the institution of the Eucharist and priesthood, but it receives it in a new way, i.e., in the light of Vatican II's teaching about the scope of the *potestas sacra* received in ordination. This explains the qualification given to the relation between the ministerial priesthood and the Eucharist. Through the phrase "principal and central *raison d'être* of the priesthood" which it uses to qualify this relation, *Dominicae Cenae* implies that the essence of the *ordo sacerdotalis* cannot be defined exclusively in terms of the Eucharist.

One other remark on Trent's canon is relevant here. The wording does not make absolutely clear how *instituisse* is to be understood in relation to the memorial command.[17] The passage of the *doctrina* which corresponds to canon 2 seems to favor the view that by the act of giving the sacred species to the apostles Christ made them priests. Hence the command "Do this . . ." is made the explicitation of the will of Christ that the apostles and their successors in the priesthood should take up the ministry of the Eucharistic sacrifice.[18] *Dominicae Cenae* repeats the position of the *doctrina.* This is shown not only from the "at the moment of . . . and together with it" (*ortum semel . . . unaque cum ea*) but also from the link placed between the institution of the priesthood and the memorial command. The letter reads: "Not without reason the words 'Do this in memory of me' are said immediately after the form (*forma*) of the Eucharistic consecration, and we repeat them every time we celebrate the holy sacrifice."

While a connection is established between the memorial command and the institution of the apostles as priests by *Dominicae Cenae,* two things are worthy of attention. First, a direct relation between the command and the historical Jesus is not explicitly affirmed in the text. The remark that the words "are said" (*prolata sunt*) could be an appeal to the New Testament Church's persuasion that it was following the intention of Christ.[19] Second, a footnote cites a liturgical source which relates the "precept of the Lord" to the establishment of the ministry of the Eucharist. *Dominicae Cenae* explains that, according to the Ethiopian anaphora of St. Athanasius, the apostles were motivated by the command to establish "patriarchs, archbishops, priests and deacons to celebrate the ritual of your holy Church."[20] The appeal to the liturgical tradition to establish a connection between the memorial command and the ordination of ministers of the Eucharist coincides with the thinking of the Council of Trent. It, too, grounds the relation on tradition.[21]

The ancient practice by which the newly ordained bishop acts as chief celebrant of the Eucharist immediately after ordination is also adduced to show the "singular and exceptional way" that the ministerial priesthood is associated with the Eucharist.[22]

Consequences of the Relationship between Eucharist and Priesthood. Two consequences are drawn from this witness of Scripture and tradition. On the one hand there exists a multiple relationship between Eucharist and priest. The ministerial priesthood *derives from it* (=originates with the institution of the Eucharist), *exists for it* (=principal reason for the existence of the sacrament of the priesthood), and has certain responsibilities *concerning it.* The last relation is based on the pastoral mission of office. Thus *Dominicae Cenae* distinguishes between the giving of the Eucharist to the whole Church and the transmission of it to priests "for" the others. Because of this mission of priests, the laity can expect that they will exhibit a "special witness of veneration and love for the sacrament" which has the effect of deepening the devotion of the laity so that they too may offer "spiritual sacrifices."[23]

The second consequence is a development of the first. The "eucharistic cult" of priests, both in the celebration of the Eucharist and outside it, is the "life-giving current which links our ministerial priesthood to the common priesthood of the faithful and presents the latter (*illud*) in its vertical dimension and with its central value." In short, the identity of the priest is revealed in the celebration of the Eucharistic sacrifice since he "fulfills his principal mission and is manifested in all his fullness when he celebrates the Eucharist." But this manifestation is more complete "when he himself allows the depth of the mystery to become visible." This is the "supreme exercise of the 'kingly priesthood.' " *Dominicae Cenae* thus teaches that the fulfillment of the priestly ministry of the Eucharist reaches its perfect stature when the personal Eucharistic devotion of the priest provides inspiration by which the laity, in the exercise of their common priesthood, are drawn into the same movement.

Dominicae Cenae underscores the distinctive responsibility of the clergy for the Eucharist in this pericope. In chapter 12, which treats of the Eucharist as the common possession of the whole Church, again the responsibility of the hierarchical ministry is mentioned in the remarks about the style of participation and celebration. But the letter does not envision the Eucharist as the exclusive responsibility of the ordained. The statement that priests are responsible "in a special way" (2.1), in virtue of the pastoral office, should not be understood to mean that they have a greater qualitative responsibility vis-à-vis the laity. To draw that conclusion would be just as incorrect as to say that clerics have a greater qualitative intensity and superior responsibility for the mission of the whole Church.[24]

The different responsibilities of laity and ordained for the Eucharist relate to the different roles which they have in the liturgy and other dimensions of Church life. *Dominicae Cenae* underlines the pastoral responsibility and the influence that the good example of pastors can have on the spiritual life of the Church. Still it must not be forgotten that in specific instances the witness of the laity has often had a very telling influence on the intensification of the Eucharistic devotion of the Church. A glance at the history of spirituality of the Western Church shows this.[25]

Ch. 3: The Cult of the Eucharistic Mystery.

The expression "mystery of the Eucharist" is used in Vatican II to describe the content of chapter 2 of the *Constitution of the Sacred Liturgy*.[26] It serves as a synonym for "the most holy sacrifice of the Mass."[27] However, in *Dominicae Cenae* the term has a more ample meaning. The notion of cult in the letter sometimes designates either the Eucharistic celebration itself or the cult rendered to the Eucharist at Mass and outside of it, or both at the same time. The first meaning of cult corresponds to that found in *Lumen Gentium* 28.1, i.e., the cult which consists in the celebration of the Eucharist. This contrasts with the cult of the Eucharist (objective genitive), i.e., the cult rendered to the sacramental body and blood of Christ at Mass and outside it. In chapter 3 of *Dominicae Cenae* both meanings are intended. These themes receive some development: (1) the relation of the Eucharist to Christ and the Trinity; (2) the content of Eucharistic cult which includes extra-liturgical adoration of the Eucharist.

The Addressees of Eucharistic Cult. This cult is directed "in the first place" to the Father, but it is also offered to the Son "in the Spirit." It is well known that the ancient liturgies accentuated prayer to the Father through Christ.[28] A change took place in the West in reaction to Arian theology. More emphasis was placed on prayer to the Son after the fourth century.[29] But there also exists in the Byzantine tradition a long history of liturgical piety directed to Christ which was not influenced by the Arian controversy.[30] The *Constitution on the Sacred Liturgy* of Vatican II offers a concise statement of the balanced approach that should be taken to this question in view of the whole liturgical tradition of the Church: "The Church is his beloved bride who calls to her Lord, and through him offers worship to the eternal Father."[31] *Dominicae Cenae* follows this lead, accentuating worship of Christ while at the same time calling attention to the Trinitarian dimension of the liturgy.

The Content of Eucharistic Cult. The cult of the Eucharistic mystery, directed to the Son, is focused on his voluntary death to which the words of institution of the Eucharist refer.[32] *Dominicae Cenae* recalls the liturgical expression of this, i.e., the acclamation "We announce your death . . ." placed after the form of consecration. The letter explains that while the acclamation includes a confession of Christ's resurrection and coming in glory, it is "the voluntary death (*exinanitio*), accepted by the Father and glorified with the resurrection, which, sacramentally celebrated together with the resurrection, brings us to adore the Redeemer who 'became obedient unto death, even death on a cross.' "[33]

This rather clumsy sentence is inspired by the hymn of Philippians 2:6–11 as the quotation of verse 8 indicates. According to the scriptural text Christ possessed divinity before the incarnation (6) but concealed his mystery during his earthly life (7).[34] Out of obedience to the Father he accepted the human condition even unto death (8). The Father responded by exalting him and giving his own name to Jesus, i.e., revealing to the world that he is both Savior and Lord (9). Therefore everyone identifies the name of Jesus with Lord and adores him as both Savior and Lord (10–11).

The cult of the crucified Savior, which the liturgy proclaims, leads *Dominicae Cenae* to comment on the greatness of Christ's "human death." It reveals a love for each person and provokes a response of thanksgiving. Hence adoration of Christ takes the form of *eucharistia,* i.e., "our giving thanks to him, our praise of him for having redeemed us by his death. . . ." This adoration, it is concluded, should also be offered to the reserved species in the various forms of Eucharistic devotion approved by the Church.[35] Moreover it should be characterized by a readiness "to make reparation for the great faults and crimes of the world."[36] *Dominicae Cenae* does not pause to explain theologically the relationship of cult offered outside Mass to that offered in the Mass. But the intimate link is implied in the description of both forms of worship.

Ch. 4: Eucharist and Church.

This pericope is built around two formulas: (1) "The Church makes the Eucharist; the Eucharist makes the Church";[37] (2) the Eucharistic sacrifice is the "source and summit" of the whole of Christian life.[38]

The Eucharist Makes the Church. The point of departure for the first theme is the significance of the "mystery of Holy Thursday." The letter explains that from the moment the apostles entered "into sacramental Communion with the Son of God," the Church "builds itself up by the same Communion with the Son of God." The Last Supper is thus set squarely within the final process of the founding of the Church which includes the death and resurrection of Christ together with the sending of the Holy Spirit. *Dominicae Cenae* does not say that the action of the Last Supper coincides with the full realization of the Church. But it does affirm that the first sacramental Communion occurred here.[39]

The gathering of the apostles around Christ at the Last Supper and participation in Eucharistic Communion is viewed as the prototype of the spiritual drawing together and union of Christians that takes place in the Eucharist.[40] For the Church is "brought together" when Christians "celebrate the sacrifice of the cross of Christ . . . and later, when . . . we approach as a community the table of the Lord . . . (to) receive Christ himself." It is this union with Christ which brings it about that "we are also associated in the unity of his body which is the Church."

The Eucharist: Source and Summit of Church Life. The second quotation from Vatican II, concerning the Eucharist as the "source and summit" of Church life, is associated with similar ideas found in the collect of the Mass of Holy Thursday and the *epiclesis* of Communion of the second Eucharistic Prayer of the New Missal. It resonates with the Augustinian teaching about the mystery of the Church as the content of the Eucharist.[41] This characteristic of the Eucharist leads *Dominicae Cenae* to infer "the direct relationship between the Church's spiritual and apostolic vitality and the Eucharist, understood in its profound aspects and from all points of view."

Within the two formulas the notion of the Eucharist "making the Church" or "source" of the Church has deep roots in tradition. In patristic exegesis the Johannine account of the water and blood flowing from the side of Christ (Jn. 19:34; 1 Jn. 5:6–8) is understood to symbolize the birth of the Church since the elements signify baptism and Eucharist by which the Church is "made." The Western Church repeated this teaching down through the twelfth century.[42] However since the thirteenth century, and paralleling the obscuring of the ecclesial dimension of baptism and the growing intensity of Eucharistic devotion, greater emphasis was placed on the role of the Eucharist to make the Church.

The Reception of the Council of Trent's Teaching on the Relationship of the Last Supper to the Cross. It is noteworthy that this chapter contrasts the relationship of the Last Supper and Mass to the cross. The sacramental Communion of the apostles at the Last Supper is viewed as "a pledge of eternal life" (4.1). The sacramental Communion in the Mass is also awarded an eschatological aspect: "pledge of the eternal Passover." But in addition the Mass is seen as the celebration of the "sacrifice of the cross" and the participants of Holy Communion at Mass are said to share in "the fruits of the holy propitiatory sacrifice" (4.3). In 9.6 a reference is also made to the propitiatory character of the Eucharistic sacrifice. Nowhere is the Last Supper awarded this title.

No doubt *Dominicae Cenae* follows the lead of the Fathers at
the Council of Trent who decided not to attempt to resolve the question of the propitiatory nature of the Last Supper. In the *doctrina,*
chapter 1, of Trent's *Decree on the Mass,* Christ is understood to
have made an offering ordered to the cross.[43] The prevailing concept
of sacrifice at Trent, drawn from Old Testament models, enabled the
Fathers not only to speak of Christ's offering at the Last Supper as
a sacrifice, but also to ask: Was it a sacrifice in the full sense? A significant number of the Fathers hesitated on this point because it was
not evident that the propitiatory aspect, traditionally linked to the
cross, could be predicated of the Last Supper. This problematic explains why the *doctrina* merely states that Christ offered himself and,
incidentally, why the offering of the New Testament priests is exclusively linked to the sacrifice of the cross, i.e., is considered to be the
representation of the cross. It also explains why nothing is said
about Christ's offering at the Last Supper in canon 2 of this session.[44]

Canon 1 of this session of Trent describes the Mass as a "true
and proper sacrifice" (*verum et proprium sacrificium*).[45] It rejects the
opinion that the Mass merely affords the opportunity to share in the
fruits of the historical sacrifice of Christ. It also judges inadequate
the narrow katabatic view that the Mass is simply our thanksgiving.
This view was not considered to be in harmony with either the meaning of the unique sacrifice offered by Christ as the head of redeemed
mankind on the cross or with the mystery dimension of Christian existence. Finally this canon is open to a more profound interpretation
of the intimate relation between Holy Communion and the sacrifice
of the Mass. The connection is indicated in the *doctrina,* chapter 1,
which explains this canon. The phrase "to consume" (*ut sumerent*)
relativizes the opposition between the holy food and the sacrificial
act as does the reference to the food sacrifice ("pure oblation,"
munda oblatio) of Malachi.[46]

In canon 3 of this session the "true and proper sacrifice" (*verum
et proprium sacrificium*) is identified with "propitiatory sacrifice"
(*sacrificium propitiatorium*).[47] This canon affirms that the sacrifice of
the Mass contains an offering of Christ which represents the offering
of the cross. Therefore not the subjective recall of the Church, but
the presence of Christ as offerer and offered is crucial. In addition

this canon refuses to limit the meaning of the represented offering to those who receive Communion: it is profitable for the living and dead in many ways. Finally by rejecting the qualification of the Mass as "only an action of praise and thanksgiving" (*tantum laudis et gratiarum actionis*) it leaves open the way to a richer interpretation of the subjective participation of the community. Canon 4 which follows serves to prevent the use of models of concurrence, addition, etc., to be applied to the relation between cross and Mass. It teaches that precisely the sacrifice of the cross is represented and applied in the Mass.[48]

But the Last Supper is not so qualified in the *Decree on the Mass*. It could therefore be understood, as a number of Fathers explained at Trent, as an ingredient of Christ's total offering of self during his earthly life which culminated on the cross.[49] While *Dominicae Cenae* displays the same reticence as that shown at Trent in the approach to the relation between the Last Supper and cross, in section II the Last Supper offering in which Christ "pledged to give his life for us" is described as an act in which he "celebrated sacramentally the mystery of his passion and resurrection" (8.3). The discussion of the extent to which this viewpoint goes beyond that of Trent is deferred to the commentary on that chapter.

In a series of further reflections the horizontal dimension of the Eucharistic sacrifice and Communion is explored under the themes of charity, neighbor and life.

Ch. 5: Eucharist and Charity.

This passage is a development of the *epiclesis* of Communion of the Eucharistic Prayer, cited at the end of chapter 4, which asks that the Lord "perfect the Church in charity." The Eucharistic celebration, which represents the sacrifice of the cross, signifies the love of God and neighbor, "recalls it, makes it present and at the same time brings it about." It recalls God's love for us and so leads to a worship that springs from love and to a response of love of God and neighbor through the "free gift, which is charity."

Ch. 6: Eucharist and Neighbor.

Here one educative effect of the rite of Eucharistic Communion is mentioned. Since Christ offers himself equally to all in the sacrament, it makes the participants aware "of the dignity of each person." This becomes the "deepest motive of our relationship with our neighbor." Who can be indifferent to all human suffering when it is discovered that the inner self becomes "the dwelling place of God present in the Eucharist"?

Ch. 7: Eucharist and Life.

This chapter begins by calling attention to another educative effect of the Eucharist derived from the way it symbolizes the intimate relation between God and mankind. The symbolism of the Eucharist, food and drink, promotes veneration of God who, by analogy with food and drink, nourishes the participants inwardly. According to *Dominicae Cenae* the whole sacramental style of Christian life springs from this understanding of Eucharistic worship. Since the Eucharist fosters an attitude of intimacy between the believer and God, Christians are led to desire God to act on them in order that they may be enabled to attain, "in the Spirit, 'the fullness of Christ himself.' " This desire conforms to God's intention who "acts on them with greater certainty and power through the sacraments."[50]

The link between the Eucharist and other sacraments, a popular theme in Scholastic theology, is also briefly described. The Eucharist draws out the meaning of baptism: the fact that one is a child of God is dramatically expressed in the Communion of the body and blood of the Son of God. The challenge of confirmation to be a "witness of Christ" is expressed in the Eucharist where not only Christ witnesses to us but "we to him."

Special attention is given to the relationship between the sacrament of penace and the Eucharist. The "sacrament of penance" leads to the Eucharist but also the "sense of unworthiness" fostered by the Eucharist leads to penance. Here the comment is made that the practice of the virtue of penance and the sacrament of penance are necessary to deepen the spirit of veneration. The reference to the intimate relation between the virtue of *metanoia* and the sacrament of *metanoia* points to the proper effect of the sacrament when one has recourse to it not from the necessity of reconciling oneself with the Church and God but in order to intensify the *metanoia* that undergirds the whole life of the Christian in the pilgrimage toward God.

Section I closes with a cryptic statement about the relationship between the commitment undertaken toward humanity and the Church in Eucharistic Communion and the deepening of love for others that is the effect of the Eucharist. This relation is regarded as the starting point for a description of how the transformation of all that is human takes place in the Eucharist.[51]

Section II:
The Sacred Character of the Eucharist and Sacrifice.

As was previously noted, the plan of the letter follows the basic structure of the post-Tridentine Scholastic systematic theology of the Eucharist. The chronological order in which Trent treated the essential aspects of the Eucharist corresponds to this systematic elaboration: sacrament (sess. xiii), Communion (sess. xxi), and sacrifice (sess. xxi–xxii). Various extrinsic reasons account for this. However it is doubtful whether, even if the ordering had been changed, the Fathers at Trent would have been able to construct a more satisfactory doctrine of the unity of the Eucharistic mystery.

The Tridentine and Post-Tridentine Approach to the Unity of the Eucharistic Mystery. Sixteenth century Scholastic theology had inherited a theology of the Eucharist whose roots can be traced back to the Carolingian period. Characteristic of this theology is the playing off of religious symbols against the mystery signified. The ninth century problematic in the matter of Eucharistic theology is the same for both Paschasius Radbertus and Ratramnus of Corbie whose writings represent a traditional and modern approach: What is the relation between the truth (*veritas*) and its sign (*figura*) in the mystery of the Eucharist?

Paschasius, more attentive to the old tradition, maintains the unity between the symbols of Christ's body and blood and the objective presence of the crucified and risen Savior together with the unity of the sacrifice of the Mass and cross. The consecrated bread and wine are the body and blood: the memorial and sacrifice of the Church contains the mystery of the sacrifice of the cross. On the other hand, Ratramnus so opposes symbol and reality that the link between the sacrament of the body and blood and the presence of Christ is not one of an inward unbroken relation. Furthermore the memorial of the sacrifice of the cross is understood as a subjective memorial since the event of the cross lies in the past.

In the ensuing three centuries the debate over the relationship of the sacrament of the body and blood to the risen Lord resulted in a clear confession of the inner unity between symbol and real presence. This was supported by the doctrine of transubstantiation which was not based on a theology of religious symbols. However the inner relation between the sacrifice of the Mass and that of the cross was not grounded on the mystery presence of the cross in the Mass. The sacrifice of the Mass was understood as an outward and purely figurative representation of the passion of Christ. The sacramental signs of the separated body and blood, which signify Christ's death, were contrasted with the sacramental real presence of Christ who offered himself on the cross. This sacramental presence of Christ secured the sacramental real relation between the cross and Mass.

The whole of sixteenth century Catholic theology accepted this point of view. Thus in all the systematic approaches the presence of Christ in the sacrament, as the same sacrificial gift on the altar and cross, provided the starting point for the explanation of the sacrificial character of the Mass. Since the unique sacramental real content of the sacrament was understood to be Christ abstracted from his once for all sacrifice accomplished on the cross, the sacrificial nature of the Mass could not be adequately explained simply from the sacrament. Rather it depended on the proof that the priest, who celebrates the Mass, offers the sacramental body and blood of Christ. This outlook continued in Catholic theology down to the twentieth century.[52]

The Ordering of Sacrifice and Sacrament in Modern Catholic Theology. The problem of the ordering of sacrament to sacrifice in a systematic way has attracted the attention of theologians ever since the Council of Trent. Through developments which have occurred during this century a new synthesis has been attained in Catholic theology.[53] Modern Catholic theologians favor a liturgical approach inspired by the great themes of the Eucharistic Prayer—thanksgiving-praise, *epiclesis,* memorial—and by the awareness of the presence of the mystery of the sacrifice of the cross in the Eucharistic celebration.

In the newer approach one moves from the concept of sacramental sacrifice to that of sacrificial sacrament, but not in such a way that the sacrificial action is simply separated from the meal, the sharing of the holy food. The Mass is understood to contain the sacramental re-presentation of the mystery of the sacrifice of the cross. The sacrament of the real presence originates from this sacramental sacrifice and bestows its fruits on the communicants. But the whole sacrificial act is not symbolically represented simply by the consecratory act of the priest! The sacramental symbolic form that proclaims the presence of Christ's sacrifice is the liturgical recitation of the account of institution of the Eucharist. The sacramental symbolic gesture, or action, which represents and applies this sacrifice to the participants is the sharing of the meal.

Dominicae Cenae accepts the point of view that the sacrificial sacrament originates from the representation of the sacrifice of the cross. But it does not show how the consecration of the gifts of bread and wine and the sharing of the sacramental body and blood form together the one unique symbolic representation of the self-offering of Christ to the Father on behalf of mankind. The Eucharist is declared to be "above all else a sacrifice" (9.1). The sacrificial action is, however, exclusively referred to the consecratory act of the priest. The priest offers "in the person of Christ (*in persona Christi*) . . . in specific sacramental identification with the 'eternal High Priest' " (8.4). Therefore the active presence of Christ the High Priest, offering his sacrifice of the cross, is the grounds for the existence of the permanent sacrament which gives to the sacrifice of the Mass the form of a sacrificial meal. The reception of the permanent sacrament is the means ordered by Christ for a more perfect sharing in the graces of the mystery of the sacrifice of the cross which is represented and re-presented in the consecration of the bread and wine. Holy Communion, therefore, is not an end to which the re-presentation of the historical sacrifice of the cross is subordinated. Rather it is a privileged moment of the sacramental encounter with the crucified and risen Lord which begins with the sacramental re-presentation of the cross through the consecration of bread and wine.

The Sacramental Rite of the Last Supper. A conceptual difficulty arises from the qualification by *Dominicae Cenae* of the nature of the apostles' Communion at the Last Supper as *sacramental* (4.1). A similar difficulty arises from the statement that on this occasion "Christ, by pledging to give his life for us, himself celebrated sacramentally the mystery of his passion and resurrection" (8.3). Since the same adjective and adverb are used to qualify Holy Communion in the time of the Church (4.2; 4.3) and the ritual act of the Mass (3.2), does this mean that *Dominicae Cenae* offers a new approach to the relationship of the cross to the Last Supper and Mass?

A partial response to this question has already been given. In section I the kernel of the Last Supper is described as including (1) an offering of Christ that points to the sacrifice of the cross but does not realize the propitiatory fruits of the cross; (2) a sacramental Communion with Jesus Christ as pledge of eternal life but not a sharing in the propitiatory fruits of the cross. Thus if the letter refers to the offering of Christ and Communion of the apostles as *sacramental,* the qualification is not precisely the same as when applied to the Mass.

In the time of the Church the sacramental sacrifice exists in order that the Church might be drawn into the mystery of the cross which is re-presented and so offer itself in a liturgical way in union with the crucified and risen Lord. The sacrificial sacrament exists as a means of a more profound personal communion with the same Lord who, existing outside the confines of time and space, must make himself personally present in history by way of the preaching of the Word of God, celebration of the sacraments, and the lives and good works of believers.

Scholastic theologians of the sixteenth century could argue, as some did at the Council of Trent, that the Last Supper represented the sacrifice of the cross to the extent of being a propitiatory sacrifice. This was possible because of the contemporary understanding of sacrifice based on Old Testament models. Thus, for example, in the General Congregation of the Council of Trent, August 19, 1562, the bishop of Leros reasoned that Christ offered a propitiatory sacrifice at the Last Supper because he offered something. His argument was based on the definition of sacrifice given by St. Thomas: "As often as something is offered to God, which is killed, eaten or drunk, it is a true sacrifice" (S.T. II/II, q. 85, a. 1).[54] The unity of the Last Supper and cross, just as is true of the unity of the cross and the Mass, was considered sufficiently secured because of the sacramental presence of Christ as offerer and offered.[55]

This option is not open to modern Catholic theology which recognizes the need to integrate the patristic understanding of the mystery presence of the sacrifice of the cross into an adequate theological explanation of the sacrifice of the Mass. Today there is a better awareness that the uniqueness of the Mass cannot be explained merely on the basis of the presence of Christ, priest and victim. While the novelty of the sacrifice of Christ and the Church consists in the identification of offerer and offered, the mystery of the sacrifice of the Mass includes the presence of Christ offering the once for all sacrifice which culminated on the cross in the memorial rite of the Church. It also includes the offering of the community which, in the power of the Spirit, is enabled to bind itself to the one living sacrifice of Christ re-presented in the rite of the bread and cup and so worship the Father in an acceptable way.

In this purview the offering made by the historical Jesus at the Last Supper in the rite of the bread (and cup?) is a symbolic expression of his sacrificial dispositions: his devotion to the Father in obedience and love which was displayed throughout the whole of his life. It can be called a ritual offering or, as *Dominicae Cenae* says, "a sacred rite" (8.3). Moreover it can be qualified as a *sacramental* celebration of the mystery of the passion and resurrection (8.3), according to the meaning of the words "sacrament," "sacramental" and "sacramentally" in *Dominicae Cenae*.

In *Dominicae Cenae* the word "sacrament" designates (1) the consecrated species: "blessed sacrament" (2.4; 3.4; 5.1); "sacrament of love" (3.5); "great sacrament" (11.4); "sacrament of the Eucharist" (7.5); "sacrament" (7.1; 7.3); (2) the whole Eucharistic mystery: "greatest gift of the order of grace and sacrament" (12.1); "sacrament of unity" (12.2); "sacrament ... source of unity" (13.5); (3)

other principal rites of the Church: "sacraments of Christian initiation: baptism and confirmation" (7.3); "sacrament of penance" (7.4; 7.5); "sacrament of the priesthood" (2.2). In all cases the word "sacrament" expresses the "objective sacred character" (8.7) of the permanent sacrament of the Eucharist, the whole Eucharistic mystery and other principal rites of the Church.

The adjective "sacramental" is employed to describe: (1) the meaning of the sharing of bread and wine at the Last Supper: "sacramental Communion with the Son of God" (4.1); (2) the meaning of Holy Communion in the time of the Church: "sacramental encounter . . . with Christ" (4.2); "nourished . . . in a sacramental way" (4.3); (3) the relation of the priest to Christ in the exercise of the ministry: "specific sacramental identification" (8.4); (4) the Eucharistic rite: "sacrificial and sacramental nature" (8.5); (5) the presence of the mystery of the cross in the Mass: "sacramental unbloody manner" (9.6); "sacramental form on the altar" (9.7); (6) the Christian style of life: "sacramental style" (7.2); "sacramental and ecclesial form" (7.3); "sacramental life" (7.3). "Sacramental" is used to indicate the affinity between authentic Christian life and the sacraments. Otherwise it refers to the objective sacred character of the principal rites of the Church and of the exercise of the ministry of the hierarchical priesthood.

The adverb "sacramentally" is used to describe: (1) the nature of the memorial celebration of the Mass: "voluntary death . . . sacramentally celebrated together with the resurrection" (3.2); (2) the "sacred rite" of the Last Supper: "Christ, by pledging to give his life for us, celebrated sacramentally the mystery of his passion and resurrection" (8.3); (3) Christ's presence under forms of bread and wine: "sacramentally present" (3.4); (4) the effect of the ordination rite: "sacramentally consecrated" (11.9). Thus it expresses the objective sacred character of the species of bread and wine or the action described by "celebrated" and "consecrated."

As expressive of the sacred character of Jesus' action at the Last Supper the phrase "sacramentally celebrated" points to its redemptive meaning. This can also be predicated of all Jesus' human activity during the course of his earthly life which, as a whole, makes up his redemptive work. But the qualification must not be understood to mean that by way of anticipation the mystery of the particular act which culminated Jesus' historical existence—the historical offering of the cross—is re-presented at the Last Supper. This can only be predicated of the Mass.

Modern Catholic theology has no difficulty with qualifying the Last Supper offering as "sacramental," i.e., as possessing an intrinsically sacred character. This also holds for the symbolic action by which Christ shared the bread and wine with the apostles as the expression of his desire to incorporate them into his response to the Father. However, in the latter case the qualification "sacramental" is awarded a meaning which corresponds to the existential state of Jesus who "had not yet been glorified" (Jn. 7:39b). In the time of the Church it is the pneumatic Christ who communicates himself to believers in the power of the Spirit through the ministry of priests.

An Exegetical Approach to the Relationship of the Last Supper to the Cross and Mass. From the standpoint of historical exegesis a difficulty arises concerning Jesus' own self-understanding of the meaning of his surrender to the will of the Father and his gesture of communicating himself to the apostles through the rite of the bread and cup.

One can certainly accept as historically probable, on the basis of New Testament exegesis, that Jesus, acting on human knowledge, was quite aware of the serious threat to his life when he met with the disciples for the evening meal during Passover week. It is also probable that he spent many hours reflecting on this situation and came to the conclusion that his time had come for death and that, in God's plan, it was a necessary stage leading to the fulfilled kingdom. In this situation in which the in-breaking of the kingdom is delayed, and in view of the denial of his message which is from God and his premonition of death, he accepts the will of the Father and recognizes that the offering of himself to God "for the many" has the expiatory meaning which is described in Isaiah 52–53 and associated with the sufferings of the "just man" in the Jewish writings of the Diaspora. But what can be said about Jesus' own sacramental understanding of the act of distribution of the bread and wine?

The notion of sacrament in the narrow sense pertains to the Hellenistic and not to the Semitic conceptual world. A particular way of personal self-mediation through a special kind of meal ingredient cannot be derived directly from Semitic thinking. But we must reckon with the fact that at the time of Jesus the Hellenistic and Semitic worlds had many points of contact and of mutual influence. Moreover if one absolutizes the principle of derivation from the contemporary context and considers only that to be historically authentic which can be otherwise verified in the immediate historical context, then the uniqueness of Jesus himself becomes unexplainable. Only under the presupposition that Jesus in his actions and thinking transcended the usual and known can a sacramental understanding of the Last Supper action be attributed to him. There seems to be no historical objection that completely nullifies this possibility. But more can be said on the basis of the history of tradition of the accounts of institution of the Eucharist.

It is historically credible that Jesus gave the bread at the outset of the meal to his disciples in order to demonstrate his conviction of the positive meaning of his death and to draw them into his saving action. Along with the gesture, he interprets the meaning of the distribution with words that most certainly go back to the Last Supper: "This is my body (=my whole person)." That this statement was qualified by a reference to the expiatory nature of his self-offering— "given for many"—also seems certain.

At the end of the meal, whatever may be said about the history of the tradition of the cup words, Jesus must certainly have reiterated the finality of this meal at the drinking of the cup by referring to the imminent death while stressing the promise of the fulfilled kingdom. This is shown from Mark 14:25 which, in the opinion of most scholars, represents an authentic word of Jesus spoken at the Last Supper.[56]

The Major Concern of Section II. While *Dominicae Cenae* provides a formulation of the theology of the Eucharistic sacrifice in which the relation of the sacrificial action to the permanent sacrament follows the main lines of contemporary Catholic theology, the overriding concern of section II is not precisely that of the systematic theologian. The centrality of this section is indicated not only by its place in the letter but also by the opening and closing sentences of the latter part of section I, chapters 5–7. From the point of view of systematic theology there was no need to preface the reflection on the horizontal dimension of the Eucharistic mystery with the remark that it is introduced "before proceeding to more detailed observations on the subject of the celebration of the holy sacrifice" (5.1). Moreover the closing paragraph of chapter 7 situates what follows in a new perspective. Here it is stated that the Sacred Congregation for the Sacraments and Divine Worship will issue a special instruction on the subject of the celebration of the Eucharistic sacrifice.

The central concern of section II, which serves as point of departure for the new instruction, is: what is "essential and immutable in the Eucharistic mystery" (9.1) and what elements are subject to change. The need to discuss this question arose from the criticism of the New Mass of Paul VI. Some traditionalist Catholics, who form a significant minority, have challenged Paul VI's claim that an "uninterrupted tradition"[57] has been maintained between the renewed liturgy and the Mass of Paul V (= the Tridentine Mass). In their estimation the latter alone secures the organic unity with the theology and practice of the united Church of the first millennium. *Dominicae Cenae* addresses this problem, reassuring those who are disturbed by the extent of the reform and its orthodoxy and showing the benefits of the "renewed liturgy."

Ch. 8: The Sacred Character of the Eucharist.

The first of the "essential and immutable" aspects of the Eucharistic liturgy is its intrinsic holiness which derives from the presence and action of Christ. As a consequence of this holiness, the priest celebrant must be understood as one who acts *in persona Christi.* In his official role, during the Liturgy of the Word, the priest represents Christ who enters the sanctuary and proclaims the Gospel. In the Eucharistic liturgy he represents Christ who is both priest and victim. Here *Dominicae Cenae* quotes an ancient textual variation of the Great Entrance prayer of the Byzantine liturgy which states that Christ is "the offerer and offered, the consecrator and consecrated." This quotation from the Codex Barberini Gr. 366 (eighth century) is a variation found in only one other recension of the *Nemo dignus* prayer.[58] The *textus receptus* reads: ". . . the one who offers and is offered, who accepts and is distributed."

It is probable that the Barberini version existed alongside the *textus receptus* as a different redaction. This is significant, for it shows that the understanding of Christ as consecrator was not viewed as incompatible with the similar role ascribed to the Holy Spirit in the early Byzantine liturgical invocation of the Spirit to consecrate the gifts (= the *epiclesis* of consecration placed after the account of institution of the Eucharist in the Eucharistic Prayer). Hence this liturgical witness offers one point of departure for a discussion between the Orthodox and Roman Catholic Churches over the relationship of Christ and the Spirit to the Eucharistic consecration.[59]

The formula *Sancta sanctis* of the Antiochene Liturgy of St. John Chrysostom, which refers to Christ the holy one (*Sancta*) given to the holy people (*sanctis*) in Holy Communion, is also introduced. This formula demonstrates that the Eucharistic action of the priest, who represents Christ, is a holy action because through it the sacred species are constituted.

From this liturgical witness to the meaning of the Eucharist *Dominicae Cenae* draws the conclusion that the Mass is a sacred action since it contains the action of Christ in the form of the "sacred rite" which Christ himself enacted at the Last Supper when he "celebrated sacramentally the mystery of his passion and death, the heart of each Mass." Consequently the activity of the priest at the core of every Mass can only be understood as the offering of "the holy sacrifice *in persona Christi.*" It is not something that "man adds to Christ's action in the Upper Room." Rather the priest acts "in specific sacramental identification with 'the eternal high priest.' " He is "sacramentally made part" of the holy sacrifice and so "spiritually linking with it in turn all those participating in the Eucharistic assembly."

This description of the relation of priest to Christ in the Eucharistic action reflects the *in persona Christi* theology of the ordained ministry of Vatican II, as developed in the post-Vatican II official Roman Catholic theology. As yet this theology has not been tempered by the insertion of a pneumatological approach to the theology of ordained ministry. In the international dialogue with the Orthodox Church which recently began,[60] it will certainly be given some attention.[61]

However, the main point of the pericope is the distinction between the essence of the "mystery" instituted by Christ at the Last

Supper and the "secondary elements which have undergone certain changes" in the course of centuries. Here stress is placed on the fact that the Eucharist is holy because it contains the presence and action of Christ in two ways: he is represented by the celebrant in the sacrificial offering, and through this action the sacred species are constituted. This basing of the intrinsic holiness of the Eucharist on the holiness of the Christ who is present echoes the traditional approach of the classical Western theology of the Eucharist. It also avoids the need to enter into prolonged discussion of the category of the sacred as applied to the question of the desacralization of the Church, an issue raised by traditionalist Catholics, or the debate of biblical theology concerning the originality of the New Testament concept of holiness in relation to pagan religions and the Old Testament.

Ch. 9: The Eucharistic Sacrifice.

The sacrificial character of the Eucharist as the re-presentation of the unique sacrifice of Christ is affirmed on the basis of the teaching of Trent, Vatican II, and a synod of Constantinople of 1156–1157, as well as the witness of the New Roman Missal. Thus this teaching appears as a constant doctrine of the Roman Catholic Church before and after Vatican II, as well as the theological stance of the Orthodox Church after the rupture of 1054.[62] Hence it expresses the belief of the undivided Church of the first millennium. The terminology used for the Eucharistic sacrifice in this chapter is also intended to make the same point. Vatican II's description of the Eucharist as "sacrifice of redemption" and "sacrifice of the new covenant" is placed alongside Trent's characteristic "propitiatory sacrifice." While different terms may be used in the modern Church, the same thing is meant. This should serve to restore the confidence of those who are uneasy with recent theological orientations.

Three aspects of the Eucharistic sacrifice are considered: (1) the restorative effect; (2) the offering of the Church in union with Christ; (3) the intimate link between the sacramental and sacrificial dimensions of the Eucharist.

The Restorative Effect. As sacrifice of the new covenant in which the sacrifice of Christ is present, the Eucharist is a "true sacrifice" which brings about the restoration of mankind and the world to God. This reflection affords an opportunity for the Pope to treat the relationship of the mission of the Son in the incarnation to that of the Spirit in the time of the Church, both of which have the goal of restoring mankind to loving communion with the Father. This is the place, in particular, where the Spirit's role in the Eucharistic sacrifice might have received some attention. But these themes are not introduced. The interest of the Pope lies in the formulation of the correct understanding of the different roles of priest and laity and the nature of their active participation in the Eucharistic celebration.

The Offering of the Church in Union with Christ. The distinction between the liturgical roles of the priest and laity was clearly drawn in Vatican II's *Constitution on the Church* (10.2). A paraphrase of this is given in *Dominicae Cenae*. Since the Mass is a true sacrifice the celebrant is a priest "in virtue of sacred ordination." He performs "a true sacrificial act that brings creation back to God." The laity "do not confect the sacrament as he does . . . but offer with him . . . their own spiritual sacrifices."

This last remark serves as an introduction to a new line of thought which takes inspiration from what the *General Instruction of the Roman Missal* says about the "spiritual value and meaning" of the presentation of the bread and wine at the altar[63] and the Eucharistic offering of all the participants of the Mass,[64] which echoes Vatican II's *Constitution on the Sacred Liturgy* 48. Thus a balance is struck between the concern to differentiate the liturgical roles of priest and laity and the need to affirm the Augustinian doctrine about the total body of Christ as subject of the Eucharistic offering. Preoccupation with the differentiation of liturgical roles can give the false impression that the spiritual sacrifices of the laity are somehow added alongside that of Christ's offering of himself.

Following the Augustinian teaching about the symbolism of the bread and wine, *Dominicae Cenae* says that the "spiritual sacrifices" offered in virtue of the common priesthood are "represented by the bread and wine from the moment of their presentation at the altar." They become "in a sense a symbol of all that the Eucharistic assembly brings, on its own part, as an offering to God and offers spiritually."[65] In this ambiance the value of the new offertory procession is explained. It fosters the attitude of self-offering which should be in the foreground of the community's thinking as the *Orate fratres* prayer indicates.

The link between the presentation of the gifts and the accompanying sacrificial devotion to the sacramental kernel of the Eucharist is now introduced. The attitude of self-offering finds its climactic expression "at the moment of the consecration and the anamnesis offering." This is shown by the words of the Eucharistic Prayer said aloud by the priest. *Dominicae Cenae* quotes the anamnesis offering prayer of Eucharistic Prayer III of the New Missal. This prayer relates the offering of the participants to that of Christ and petitions that through Holy Communion the participants "may be filled with the Holy Spirit, and become one body, one spirit in Christ."[66]

The Link between the Sacramental and Sacrificial Dimensions of the Eucharist. *Dominicae Cenae* goes on to explain how the bread and wine presented at the altar become a sacrifice in the strict sense, a "consecrated offering." This consecration takes place through the transformation of the species by which they become "truly, really and substantially Christ's own body that is given and his blood that is shed." Moreover it is "by virtue of this consecration" that "the species of bread and wine represent, certainly in a sacramental and unbloody way, the bloody propitiatory sacrifice offered by him on the cross to the Father."

The Reception of the Council of Trent, Session xxii, Chapter 1 of the Doctrina. The above formulation is referred to the Council of Trent's teaching about the representation of the cross in the Mass.[67] But the perspective of *Dominicae Cenae* differs to some extent from that of Trent. Session xxii, *Decretum de Missa,* chapter 1 of the *doctrina* to which *Dominicae Cenae* refers, begins with the understanding of the unique sacrifice and priesthood of Christ found in the Epistle to the Hebrews. This teaching is logically linked to a statement about Christ's institution of the Eucharist and priesthood to express the idea of Hebrews that the levitical priesthood is suppressed along with its sacrifices. But immediately a different line of thought is pursued from that of Hebrews, which describes the newness and eternal duration of Jesus' priesthood, inaugurated with his death.

The mode of argumentation of the *doctrina* indicates the concern of the circle around Cardinal Seripando who composed this chapter. It was to show that the Last Supper and Mass, in their ritual celebration, correspond to a common understanding of sacrifice and, in particular, to Old Testament types: the Passover lamb and the sacrifices of Melchizedek and Malachi, while at the same time surpassing them because of the presence of the body and blood of Christ.

As a consequence of this outlook, it is affirmed that Christ gave his body and blood to the apostles "and their successors in the priesthood in order that they offer them." Here the *doctrina* speaks on the liturgical level, the level of the outward sign.[68] On the other hand, in chapter 2 of the same *doctrina* the term *offerre* has a different meaning. It refers to the self-offering of Jesus Christ: the offering of himself in the Mass as on the cross.[69] This confusion of the ritual and dogmatic modes of speech, as well as the linkage of a common cultic concept of sacrifice with New Testament statements about the sacrifice and priesthood of Jesus Christ, led to many difficulties. The more the liturgical offering was confused with the historical offering of the sacrifice of Christ, the more theologians were led to seek the act of offering to God at the level of the sign of the liturgical action. This brought them back to a pre-Christian concept of sacrifice.

The obscuring of the distinction between the liturgical *offerre* and the historical *offerre* resulted in their identification. In recent times Roman Catholic theologians have recognized this problem. Their solution is to stress the actual presence of Christ who, as sacrificial gift and priest, offers the sacrifice of the cross and represents it through the liturgical action. While *Dominicae Cenae* does not completely transcend the terminological problem, the general outlook is that of modern Catholic theology. This can be shown from the statement that, because of the consecration, the species represent "in a sacramental unbloody manner the . . . sacrifice offered by him on the cross."

The Superiority of the New Missal of Paul VI. As this chapter began by affirming the sacrificial nature of the Eucharist, so it ends by indicating how the New Missal of Paul VI has given, "so to speak, greater visibility to the Eucharistic sacrifice." The acclamation of the community "after the elevation" is singled out in this regard. But the main emphasis is placed on the new instruction that the priest recite the Eucharistic Prayer aloud, "particularly the words of consecration." These words, spoken aloud, not only proclaim for all to hear that the mystery presence of Christ's sacrifice is being realized sacramentally but should be understood as a "call of the Lord" to the participants to offer themselves in union with him as a means of purification, particularly in view of the reception of Holy Communion.

Section III:
The Two Tables of the Lord
and the Common Possession of the Church.

In a somewhat abrupt fashion two chapters are introduced concerning the Liturgy of the Word and the rite of Holy Communion along with a third on the subject of the responsibility of all members of the Church for the Eucharist.

The Traditional Meal Imagery for the Two Parts of the Mass. Vatican II used the expressions "table of the word" and "table of the bread" to stress the dignity of the Word of God,[70] the two ministries of the priest,[71] and the relationship and importance of the two parts of the Mass.[72] The imagery of the two tables is found already in a fourth century text.[73] A century earlier the symmetry between the Liturgy of the Word and Eucharist is also described by banquet images. Origen uses the symbols of food and drink to show the relation between the Eucharist and the hearing of the Word of God.[74] He can also employ the symbol of drink alone.[75]

The Theological Integration of the Modes of Christ's Presence. In the tradition of the East and West the Liturgy of the Word has always been awarded an honored place and an independent value. But in the Eucharist it has also been understood as a way of preparing the community for its act of worship in union with Christ and for Holy Communion. The history of theology in the West shows that the notion of Christ's presence in word and sacrament gradually became obscured as Scholastic theology focused attention on the sacrament of the real presence; this took place in the wake of intense theological debate and growing Eucharistic devotion. In reaction to the Reformation theology of the Word, this preoccupation with the Eucharistic presence only increased.

In the twentieth century and for various reasons, Roman Catholic theology has been led to recognize the need for a systematic elaboration of the relationship between Word and sacrament and, in particular, the relation between the Liturgy of the Word and the Eucharist. Added stimulus in this direction was provided by Vatican II's *Constitution on the Sacred Liturgy* which called attention in a non-systematic way to the various modes of Christ's real presence in the Church.[76] A more precise theological statement of this theme is found in Paul VI's encyclical letter *Mysterium Fidei.* But even here a true theological ordering and explanation of the modes of Christ's presence is not attempted.[77] *Dominicae Cenae* also poses the question in its discussion of the "two tables." Nevertheless, just as is true with the *Constitution on the Sacred Liturgy* and *Mysterium Fidei,* it is content to accentuate the relative importance of the "table of the bread of the Lord"; it provides no new contribution to the systematic problem.

From the standpoint of systematic theology it is not sufficient to simply repeat the typically Origenist phrases "bread (drink) of the word" and "bread (drink) of the Eucharist." Rather, there is a real need to follow Origen's example in his systematic approach to the modes of communication of the soul with the Divine Logos.

Origen himself uses the imagery of food and drink to indicate the relatively superior value of the Word of God, spoken in the Church, over Eucharistic Communion. His typical argument *a minore ad majorem* is exemplified in the following quotation:

> You who customarily are present at the Divine Mysteries, know how, when receiving the body of the Lord, you guard it with great care and respect, lest any particle of it should fall. . . . But if you use such great caution . . . in preserving his body, how can you think it less guilty to have neglected the Word of God than his body.[78]

From Origen's point of view the verbal word is a more efficacious means of communication with the Logos than the sacrament of the body and blood. The spiritualizing tendency of Origen's Eucharistic thinking shows itself in two ways. First it consists in the transference of the traditional sacramental concepts to verbal realities both within and outside of the ritual Eucharist. In the former case it leads to a depreciation of the material-earthly sacramental reality and the highlighting of the verbal presence of Christ in the Eucharistic Prayer. In the latter instance a "eucharistizing" of preaching and the reading of Scripture results which is an enlarging on the Word event. Secondly, it consists in the internalizing of the saving encounter with Christ, whereby preaching and Eucharistic Communion first attain their fruition in the soul of the believer as unification of the soul with the Divine Logos.[79]

While this spiritualizing tendency of Origen, influenced by a Platonic metaphysics of knowledge, an Old Testament theology of Word, and unsettled christological questions, does not provide a suitable conceptual framework for modern Catholic theology, Origen's manner of theologizing nevertheless offers an example for a modern theology of communication of Christ which breaks away from the narrow interests of traditional Catholic sacramental theology. What is clearly needed, as exemplified in the theological problem posed by the "two tables," is a unifying systematic reflection over everything which Christian tradition can characterize as "encounter with the risen Lord." This vision of a theology of *communicatio in genere,* which supplants the Scholastic treatise *De sacramentis in genere,* provides a unique challenge to Catholic theology. Its realization could have very positive effects not only on the liturgical life of Catholics but also on relations with the churches of the Reformation.

The Table of the Bread and Cup. Two additional prefatory comments on the theme of the "two tables" will suffice before discussing the contents of chapters 11 and 12. The first concerns the omission of a reference to the cup in the meal imagery of Eucharistic Communion; the second is a parenthetical observation which touches on a pastoral aspect of the recently revived lay reception of the Eucharistic cup.

Vatican II's orientation of the "two tables" toward the bread of the Lord seems to have been influenced by the Johannine theme of the two forms of the bread of life (Jn. 6:27–58).[80] This partially ac-

counts for the saying in the *Constitution on Divine Revelation* about
the "one table of the Word of God and the body of Christ."[81] But
this perspective also reflects the extent to which the cup remains in
the background of Western consciousness because of the medieval
decision to remove it from the laity and the traditional Eucharistic
devotion, supported by the doctrine of concomitance (= the whole
Christ is present under each species), which was centered around the
reserved species of bread.

However, from the viewpoint of the Eucharistic liturgy (the
context in which *Dominicae Cenae* introduces the theme of the two
tables), it would be more precise to speak of the table of the Word
which satiates hunger and thirst (Jn. 6:35) and the table of the bread
and cup, the eating and drinking of which afford the gift of eternal
life (Jn. 6:54).

The Symbolism of Reception of Communion Under Both Species. Given the powerful influence exercised by the symbolism of the
Eucharistic cup in the first millennium as attested by Christian literature, and the effect which the removal of the cup from the laity—
together with the theology of concomitance which supported it—had
on the origin and development of the peculiar form of Western Eucharistic devotion, it is tempting to insert a series of reflections on
what might be expected from a more widespread granting of the cup
to the laity. One observation of a pastoral nature must suffice. It relates to a concern underlying much of *Dominicae Cenae:* the need for
education if the new liturgical changes are to have their desired effect.

The patristic practice of *communio sub una,* in the case of infants (cup) and the sick (reserved species of bread), was motivated
by pastoral reasons. This also holds for papal documents which
unanimously condemned the practice of receiving *sub una* at the
celebration of Mass. Pope Gelasius (492–496) gives the reason,
"Whoever breaks the unity of the one unique mystery in this way
makes himself guilty of the grave sin of sacrilege."[82]

The understanding of Communion under both species as a symbolic encounter with the dead and risen Christ, and so as a pledge
of eternal life, lies at the origin of the introduction of the *commixtio*
rite before Holy Communion, linked to the second phase of the an-

aphora, the *epiclesis.* This rite first appears in the fourth century East Syrian church. Theodore of Mopsuestia and Narsai of Nisibis inform us about its original meaning. Before the *epiclesis* of the sanctification of the gifts and the participants, Christ is symbolically represented as the one being sacrificed, "the body, broken . . . the blood shed." After the *epiclesis* the sacrificial gifts are the risen Lord, living and life-giving. The unity of the body and blood in the living Lord is symbolically represented by the gesture of mixing together a part of the consecrated bread with the wine. This rite, together with the understanding of the meaning of the *epiclesis,* calls for the reception of the Eucharist under both species so as not to break "the unity of the mystery." The most ancient *Ordo Romanus I* reflects this same understanding of the symbolism of the *commixtio:* the Communion under both species is administered immediately after the *commixtio* which takes place in silence.[83]

The loss of this symbolic perception in the Carolingian world provided the cultural background for the removal of the cup from the laity. The rational explanation, devoid of liturgical considerations, that it is the same thing to communicate under one or both species within the celebration of the Mass theologically grounded the practice of *communio sub una.*

The challenge to Church authority issued by the Bohemian barons hardened the position of the Fathers of the Council of Constance; it defended the practice of removing the cup from the laity in the decree of session xiii, January 15, 1415, which was confirmed by Martin V in 1425.[84] Except for the short-lived concessions made later to Bohemia and Germany, the Council's decision remained normative until Vatican II's *Constitution on the Sacred Liturgy* 55 opened the way to a wider use of the lay cup. However, if this change in Communion practice is to have real meaning and so escape the charge of novelty, it seems imperative that the ancient understanding of its symbolism be recovered.

Ch. 10: The Table of the Word of the Lord.

This brief chapter treats of the spiritual benefits derived from the proclamation of the Word of God through reading, chant, and homily. The comment is made that through more abundant reading of the Word of God the whole faithful can become "witnesses and participants of the authentic celebration of the Word of God," and that this Word of God begins to have its effect in a number of communities thanks to the active role of readers, cantors and choirs. All this is seen as the exercise of a "new responsibility toward the Word of God" and calls for greater attention to the quality of reading and chant.

Dominicae Cenae notes that the *General Instruction of the Roman Mass* provides some liberty in the choice of texts. But it insists that only the Word of God can be used for Mass readings. Other selections can be introduced into the homily which has as one of its goals to show the convergence between the revealed Word and noble human thought.

While defending the use of the vernacular, the letter alludes to criticism leveled against the decision to drop Latin as the one language of the Roman liturgy. *Dominicae Cenae* is sympathetic toward those who miss Latin and observes that some accommodation should be made for them "as is moreover provided for in the new dispositions." A footnote gives references to the several invitations made by Rome to take into consideration the pastoral need to celebrate or sing the Mass in Latin in certain churches, especially where there are participants of different languages.

Ch. 11: The Table of the Bread of the Lord.

Section I of *Dominicae Cenae* discussed the implications of the Eucharistic presence of Christ for the orientation of Christian worship. Section II presented a theology of the Eucharistic sacrifice and showed the value of the New Mass of Paul VI for promoting a proper understanding of the fruitful participation in this celebration. This pericope considers the rite of Holy Communion under two aspects: (1) the internal dispositions of the communicant; (2) norms to be observed in the dispensing and receiving of Holy Communion.

Conditions for Worthy Reception of the Eucharist. The exclamation of the priest before the distribution of Holy Communion, "Happy are those who are called to the supper of the Lord," evokes a comparison with the saying of one who dined with Jesus at the home of a Pharisee, "Happy is he who eats bread in the kingdom of God" (Lk. 14:15). *Dominicae Cenae* recalls this liturgical text and makes a comparison between certain Catholics and the people invited to a feast in the parable which follows in the Lukan text. Just as those who were invited found superficial reasons for absenting themselves from the feast, so also there are Catholics who are not in a sinful state and yet refrain from receiving Communion out of an exaggerated sense of unworthiness or lack of interior desire. The second type is judged to be more common in this century. Of both it is said that they do not have the proper sensitivity toward and understanding of the nature of this "sacrament of love."

This group is contrasted with others who communicate frequently. How the latter group *should be subdivided* is not altogether clear from the text. *Dominicae Cenae* notes the recent phenomenon of frequent reception of Communion by the whole assembly. It states that on some occasions "due care" has not been exercised to purify one's conscience through the sacrament of penance. There may be an allusion here to the guest of the Matthean version of the Lukan parable who comes to the wedding feast of the king's son without a "wedding garment" and who is definitively excluded from the kingdom (Mt. 22:11–14). But the phrase "due care" could refer to the need for frequent confession of devotion in order to promote purity of conscience.[85] In any case *Dominicae Cenae* contrasts those who "find nothing in their conscience nor anything according to the objective law of God" which prevents them from communicating sacramentally with those who consider the Mass *only a banquet* in which one participates "by receiving the body of Christ in order to manifest, above all else, fraternal communion."

This phenomenon of frequent Communion, *Dominicae Cenae* concludes, requires pastoral attention. Christians should be guided by respect for Christ and so prepare themselves to be a worthy abode of the sacrament. This question of worthy Communion is linked both with the practice of the sacrament of penance and also with the correct sense of responsibility for the "whole deposit of moral teaching and for the precise distinction between good and evil." This distinction is the basis for the judgment about oneself which is "an indispensable condition" for the personal decision to communicate or abstain.

Eucharistic Sharing with Christians Not in Full Communion with the Roman Catholic Church. Since *Dominicae Cenae* has in mind only those in full communion with the Roman Catholic Church, it does not discuss here the special problem of the conditions under which Eucharistic Communion can be shared with churches or individual Christians who do not live in a communion that embraces the full range of the essentials of the common life of the Roman Catholic Church. But the conditions for worthy Communion and the invitation addressed to all who are worthy must also be discussed from the perspective of the principle, "The Church makes the Eucharist; the Eucharist makes the Church."

The saying "The Church makes the Eucharist" seems to imply that visible unity, which the Eucharist signifies, is a pre-condition for Eucharistic Communion between churches. The saying "The Eucharist makes the Church" implies that the Eucharist is a means by which the unity of the Church is realized. Vatican II speaks of the Eucharist as sign and cause of the unity of the Church,[86] and opens the way to *communicatio in sacris* with the Eastern Orthodox Churches based on the depth of unity already existing between them and the Catholic Church.[87] *Dominicae Cenae* makes a passing reference, in chapter 12.3, to the various norms established after Vatican II for the admission to Holy Communion of other Christians who are not in full communion with Rome, including members of the Eastern Orthodox and Oriental Churches as well as those of the Reformation tradition.[88]

The most recent instruction of the Secretariat for the Promotion of Christian Unity, to which *Dominicae Cenae* refers, affirms that the Eucharist both signifies the full unity of the Church and is a means to this unity. However, it insists that Communion cannot be regarded as a means to be used by separated churches to lead to full ecclesiastical communion. In addition, it specifies cases where individual Christians who are not in communion with Rome can communicate. For the rest it observes that because of the special situation of the Eastern Churches, *reciprocity* in the matter of individuals is possible.[89]

The conditions for frequent Communion, as is true of those for allowing Eucharistic sharing with members of separated churches, have varied in the course of time. In the latter instance the Roman

Catholic Church does not have a tradition of "intercommunion" between churches merely at the level of the Eucharist. Moreover, the official sanctioning of the practice of communicating individual schismatics and heretics—favored under certain circumstances by some Scholastic theologians on the basis of the principle *sacramenta sunt propter homines,* and an individualistic view of sacraments and their efficacy—is a relatively recent phenomenon.

The History of the Conditions for Frequent Communion. In the ante-Nicene Church before the year 300 we have no evidence that either of the above questions was posed as a theological problem. The conditions for participation in Holy Communion were one faith expressed in word and deed, baptism, and ecclesiastical communion. Those who met these conditions were expected to communicate at the Sunday liturgy.

Direct evidence for a change in the practice of weekly Communion, both in the East and West, is found in fourth century sources. Infrequent Communion in some churches resulted from a number of causes, including an exaggerated reverence for the sacred species. In the West the rigid public penitential system encouraged the delay of baptism since it offered only one reconciliation for sinners subject to public penance. Moreover, its length precluded sinners from receiving Communion over a relatively long period of time.

In the ensuing centuries frequent Communion became increasingly rare everywhere in the united Church. This paralleled a development in which the Eucharist came to be more and more identified with the clergy. It is to the credit of Lateran Council IV (1215) that it established the law of annual confession and paschal Communion as the minimum requirement for members of the Church.[90] In the wake of this decision, which explicity linked confession to the reception of the paschal Communion, systematic theology formulated the minimal conditions for the fulfillment of the law of Easter Communion, i.e., absence of the consciousness of being in the state of mortal sin. Moreover, the failure of the decree to stipulate whether only those in serious sin were obliged to annual confession left room for theologians to argue whether and how this precept related to persons in the state of grace.

The more common opinion, favored by St. Thomas,[91] denied

any obligation. But within the Franciscan school some held that those in the state of grace were bound to confess annually.[92] This latter point of view, and more especially the development of intense devotion to the Eucharistic presence of Christ, led to a more precise formulation of the conditions for more frequent Communion. Along with the custom of previous confession which took on an absolute character, the requirement of special devotion[93] and the advice of a confessor[94] are often mentioned.

In particular, the link between confession and Communion, maintained as a rule down to the twentieth century, obstructed more frequent Communion for those without serious sin. Under Pius X the decree *Sacra Tridentina Synodus* of the Sacred Congregation of the Council affirmed that all the faithful who are not conscious of being in the state of mortal sin and have the proper dispositions could communicate frequently and even daily.[95] But the custom of linking frequent Communion to frequent confession was retained and officially encouraged.[96]

In various national and local churches which had maintained Sunday attendance, frequent confession, and Communion, a dramatic change took place just before and after Vatican II. A sharp decline in the practice of frequent or even infrequent confession was accompanied by a corresponding increase in the number of those receiving Holy Communion.

In the post-Vatican II period two important reasons for the phenomenon of the reception of Communion by the whole congregation have been the encouragement provided by Vatican II and post-conciliar documents, and the renewed liturgy which provides greater opportunity for the active participation of the laity throughout the whole celebration.

On the other hand, the persistent attempts of the Roman magisterium to maintain the link between confession and Communion have not been successful. The widespread opposition to its insistence on the practice of confession before First Communion in the case of children is but one instance of the changing climate. Moreover, the new rite of penance has not had the desired result. In no way can it be said to have produced as yet an effect comparable to the new Eucharistic liturgy. The debilitating influence of modern secular culture on the moral sense of many Catholics is one cause. But the whole blame cannot be placed here. The poor state of pastoral practice must also be mentioned.

The renewed rite of the sacrament of penance presupposes professionally qualified priests who can effectively deal with "sickness of the soul." The faithful, too, expect more than the assignment of a suitable penance and the proclamation of the forgiveness of sins. It is doubtful whether any significant change will take place in the practice of frequent confession until a significant number of priests are available who are properly equipped for this ministry. In the light of the history of pastoral practice one can ask whether all priests should be expected to be able to undertake this ministry of frequent confession. In medieval Western practice it was taken for granted that the annual confession was made to the pastor of the parish to which one belonged. Otherwise spiritual authorities advised the choice of an expert in the care of souls for one's confessor.

The Modern Phenomenon of Frequent Communion: Individual and Ecclesial Dimensions. *Dominicae Cenae* refers explicitly to the medicinal effect of Holy Communion and obliquely to its function of expressing the fraternal union of the whole local community. Both these themes deserve development.

The Medicinal Value of Frequent Communion. Vatican II's *Constitution on the Sacred Liturgy* 55 describes Holy Communion as a more perfect way of participating in the Mass. This is repeated in *Dominicae Cenae,* which also speaks of Communion as a participation in "the fruits of the propitiatory sacrifice of the cross" (4.3). But one of the main effects of the proper participation in the sacrificial action of the Mass is the awakening of the spirit of *metanoia* or conversion; this should be maintained, as *Dominicae Cenae* points out, throughout the whole liturgy. This disposition is a necessary condition for the fruitful reception of Holy Communion which, in its turn, will normally intensify one's love of God and so serve as a means of purification of sinful tendencies. Hence the effect attributed to devotional confession is one effect of the devout reception of Holy Communion. No doubt this aspect of Holy Communion needs to be stressed. To the extent that the sacrament of penance is awarded the title of "sacrament of reconciliation" in an exclusive way, the sacrificial aspect of Eucharistic worship and Holy Communion is obscured.

The Ecclesial Aspect of Holy Communion. The reception of Holy Communion is a sacramental expression of the unity of the participants with one another in Christ. It is certainly worth repeating that this holy rite denotes the human and social dimension of the corporate life of the Christian community. Precisely because of this, it is radically distinguished from any type of esoteric communion rite of mystery religions; the latter attempt to provide a dramatic representation of divine communion bereft of any historical and communitarian dimension. As in the case of all the traditional sacraments of the Church, Holy Communion symbolizes something that can be lived: a relationship of shared love in daily life. It allows the participants to play out this relationship in a symbolic act. But this rite connotes, for the eyes of faith, communion with Christ, the head of the Church, and so also communion with the Holy Spirit who binds believers to Christ in the time of the Church.

Hence the unity of the members of the local church has a more profound basis than that grounded on the human will to unite. It is based on the abiding presence of Christ in the Spirit within individuals, the source of their life of faith. But since Christ in the Spirit is the ultimate source of the unity of the Eucharistic assembly, this community cannot define itself as church except in the measure of its outreach to other Eucharistic communities. This relationship of the local Eucharistic community to the universal communion of churches is touched on in *Dominicae Cenae* 12.6, where it is stated that in the Mass not only the priest "with his community . . . is praying but the whole Church, which is thus expressing in this sacrament her spiritual unity, among other ways by the use of the approved liturgical text."

Dominicae Cenae is critical of the viewpoint which describes the Mass as "only a banquet" and which understands Holy Communion "above all else" as a manifestation of "fraternal communion." One can imagine with some justification that this remark is also intended to provide a wider horizon for those groups of like-minded Catholics who habitually participate only in the Eucharistic celebrations of their private circles. There is a danger that such groups will lose sight of the relationship of each Eucharist to Christ the head of the Church and so to all other Eucharistic assemblies. As does *Dominicae Cenae,* Vatican II had tended to focus on the universal dimension of each Eucharistic celebration.[97] Post-conciliar documents do the same. For example, *The Instruction on Mass for Special Groups* speaks of educating the faithful so that everyone "in the liturgical celebration will feel at one with his brother and in communion with the universal and local church."[98]

The theological problem of the relation of the celebration of the Eucharist to the local and universal Church received some attention just before Vatican II. Up to 1950 it was the common opinion of Catholic theology that the universal Church is the immediate subject of the celebration of the Eucharist through the priest who acts as its representative. This conclusion had been formulated at the end of the thirteenth century by Duns Scotus in order to explain why each Mass, as an act of the Church, infallibly produces blessings. He reasoned that even if the participants physically present have no devotion, the prayer of the saints throughout the world is united with the concrete celebration and so from this source graces derive from each Eucharist. This theology received further support with the gradual development in the West of a juridically conceived universal Church in which the local churches are viewed as incomplete parts.

The theology of the universal Church's role in the offering of each Eucharist was first criticized on the basis of the relationship between the liturgical act and the devotion of those physically present and participating.[99] With the advent of the newer communion ecclesiology, advocated to some extent by Vatican II, the conceptual framework for the traditional approach completely collapsed. There exists at present a consensus in Catholic theology that the universal Church participates in each Mass indirectly, i.e., through the prayers of believers which are the occasion for God's bestowal of those actual graces that foster the devotion of the participants of the liturgical act. Still it cannot be said that either Vatican II or the post-conciliar documents of the magisterium have taken sides on the question of the role of the universal Church in the offering of the Eucharistic sacrifice. This may explain the phrase "among other ways" of the above quotation from *Dominicae Cenae.*[100] However, elsewhere *Dominicae Cenae* refers to the "conscious active participation (*actuosa participatio*) of the whole Eucharistic assembly" (8.3) and to the priest, acting *in persona Christi,* spiritually linking to the holy sacrifice "all those participating in the Eucharistic assembly" (8.4). These expressions point in the direction of the more recent approach to the relation of the universal communion of churches to each Eucharist.

Dispensing and Receiving Holy Communion. *Dominicae Cenae* recalls the words of the ordination rite linked to the *traditio instrumentorum* (the handing over of the paten and cup) as well as the rite of unction of hands which is peculiar to the Western Church. Both point to the special responsibility of the priest to safeguard the dignity of the rite of Holy Communion. While the letter recognizes that in exceptional cases and for a real need laity can serve as ministers of Communion, the primary responsibility falls on priests. This is based on the fact that "by ordination they represent Christ the priest . . . (and) have become direct instruments of Christ." An important symbolic expression of this fact, according to *Dominicae Cenae,* is the Western Church's rite of anointing the hands of the priest. "To touch the sacred species and to distribute them with their own hands" is seen as a "privilege of the ordained." It indicates the "active participation (*actuosa participatio*) in the ministry of the Eucharist." Because of this symbolism others who are not ordained are only employed in this ministry when special need exists and according to the order of, first, acolytes, especially those destined for ordination, and then other laity who have been chosen and prepared.

The rite of anointing of the hands of the presbyter is mentioned in Amalar of Metz's *De ecclesiasticis officiis.*[101] It is considered to have originated in the rite of ordination of the sons of Aaron. According to Numbers 3:3 they were "anointed as priests." Amalar contends that the anointing of the head was completed by the anointing of the hands so that they could function in the priesthood. Corresponding to this rite, presbyters' hands are anointed so that they might be pure to offer the victim to God. This rite was unknown in Rome in the ninth century as attested by the letter of Nicolaus I to Rodulphus (864).[102] It appears as an insertion in the *Ordo Romanus VIII* at the beginning of the tenth century. From the *Pontificale Romano-Germanicum* it passed to the twelfth century *Pontificale Ro-*

manum.[103] Ivo of Chartres (1116) views the rite as signifying the reception of the grace to consecrate and the duty of exercising works of mercy.[104] This corresponds to the understanding of the twelfth century *Pontificale Romanum* which invokes God to consecrate and sanctify the hands that they, in turn, may consecrate and bless. *Dominicae Cenae* interprets the gesture as signifying the bestowal of power but also a special responsibility for the Eucharist.

The subject of reception of Communion in the hand receives brief consideration. *Dominicae Cenae,* while referring to reports of lack of respect shown by some communicants, places the main emphasis on the failure of some pastors to respect the freedom which the faithful have to receive Communion "on the tongue." The fact that Communion in the hand is allowed in some places does not mean that the former mode of communicating is excluded.

Ch. 12: A Common Possession of the Church.

In this chapter three themes are introduced. Under the topic sentence which speaks of the Eucharist as the "greatest gift which the Divine Spouse handed on and hands on continually to his spouse," two conclusions are drawn. The greatness of the gift shows Christ's personal confidence in the Church. This calls for trust: the exercise of fidelity toward what the Eucharist expresses in itself. Because it is a gift it calls for the expression of gratitude.

The second theme is developed from the viewpoint that the Eucharist is the common possession of the Church "as sacrament of her unity." The hierarchy has the duty to regulate the Eucharistic celebration and to respect the needs of substantial unity of the Eucharistic liturgy. Nevertheless, a certain amount of creativity is advocated. The vision is projected of the ideal situation: a new equilibrium which mediates between the legitimate concerns of the Tridentine reform in the direction of uniformity on the one hand, and the pluralism of liturgical expression of the late Middle Ages.

The final consideration centers around "the special sense of the common good of the Church" which should be displayed by the priest-celebrant of the Eucharist. This requires of the priest fidelity to the use of the approved liturgical texts, a means by which the Church expresses "her spiritual unity." He should also guard against the danger of an unhealthy individualism in the manner of celebration and avoid a narrow understanding of Eucharistic piety which is unsympathetic to the various traditional forms of Eucharistic worship.

Section IV: Conclusion

Chapter 13 singles out three subjects that represent the main thrust of the letter. An interesting formulation of the importance of the liturgical renewal is followed by a brief statement about the necessity of collaboration between Rome and the episcopal conferences. Finally, an appeal is made to Catholics not to allow the liturgical renewal to become a source of division.

In a more personal use of "we," studiously avoided previously, the Pope speaks of the "organic bond that exists between the liturgical renewal and the renewal of the whole life of the Church." Because of this connection, liturgical renewal is not only the measure but also the condition for putting into effect the teaching of Vatican II. The interaction between Church and liturgy in general is thus described in terms of the interplay between Church and Eucharist: "The Church not only acts but also expresses herself in the liturgy, lives by the liturgy and draws from the liturgy the strength for her life."

The special concern of Vatican II to take inspiration from and to preserve the liturgical heritage of the united Church of the first millennium is mentioned. This implies that substantial unity exists in the liturgical sphere between the Roman Catholic Church and the Orthodox Churches. At the same time it serves as an introduction to the final appeal for unity between Catholics on the subject of liturgical renewal. But a paragraph is inserted which speaks of the need of collaboration between Rome and the episcopal conferences in the task of promoting the liturgical life.

In an obvious allusion to the criticism leveled against the new Eucharistic Liturgy by reactionary groups, the Pope labels it a menace to Church unity and an affront to the Eucharist which is the "focal point and constitutive center . . . of the unity of the Church itself." At the same time he recalls the responsibility of all to avoid deviations from a one-sided application of the principles of liturgical reform. The liturgy should be celebrated in a "catholic" style. Opportunities should be provided to meet the legitimate spiritual needs of all participants.

Notes

1. *Acta Apostolicae Sedis* (AAS) 72 (1980), 113–148.

2. AAS 71 (1979) 395ff.

3. In modern times circular letters of Popes (− encyclicals) are designated as *litterae* or *epistulae* depending on whether they are intended for bishops of a particular region or for the whole college of bishops. They can be mainly exhortatory or doctrinal in content (cf. Paul VI, "Questa Udienza Settimanale," *L'Osservatore Romano,* August 6, 1964; Eng. tr., "The Idea of an Encyclical," *The Pope Speaks* 10 [1964–1965] 248–251). *Dominicae Cenae* is a doctrinal letter.

4. E. J. Kilmartin, *Toward Reunion: The Roman Catholic and Orthodox Churches* (New York: Paulist, 1979) 35–51.

5. *Dominicae Cenae* avoids the use of "reform"; it speaks consistently of "liturgical renewal." In this way it stresses continuity with the past.

6. Several recensions of this bull exist. This translation derives from the Latin text found in *Magnum Bullarum Romanum,* III/1 (Rome: Mainardi, 1740) 415.

7. Cf. J. Frank Henderson, "The Chrism Mass and Holy Thursday," *Worship* 51 (1977) 149–158.

8. A further description and evaluation of the reform of this liturgy is found in N. Rasmussen, "The Chrism Mass: Tradition and Renewal," *The Cathedral Reader,* ed. The Center for Pastoral Liturgy, The Catholic University of America (Washington, D.C.: USCC, 1979) 23–33.

9. "Sacramental," as qualification of sacrifice, means that the mystery of the historical sacrifice of the cross is present in the Mass; "sacrificial," as qualification of sacrament, means that the presence of Christ under the forms of bread and wine is dependent on the actual presence of Christ's self-offering which culminated on the cross.

10. Th. Schneider's recent contribution to sacramental theology provides a concise analysis of the achievements of the New Missal of Paul VI together with a survey of the French and German debate about its orthodoxy and liturgical quality (*Zeichen der Nähe Gottes: Grundriss der Sakra-*

mententheologie [Mainz: Matthias-Grünewald, 1979] 134–143). The understanding of "tradition" emerges as a central issue. Traditionalists tend to ignore the fact that what is really received from the past is received in the new context of understanding and adapted to the new situation. *Dominicae Cenae* accepts a dynamic concept of tradition as the process of handing on and reception. But it does not develop theological criteria that can be used to verify that the new understanding and adaptation are in continuity with the past stages of the process of tradition.

11. Cf. P.-M. Gy, "Le lettre *Dominicae Cenae* sur le mystère et le culte de la sainte eucharistie," *La Maison-Dieu* 141 (1980) 34, n. 66, who quotes a letter of Lefebvre of Nov. 8, 1979. This letter was published in the bulletin circulated among the members of the Fraternité sacerdotale Pius X. *Dominicae Cenae* addresses, in one way or another, almost all of the objections to the Mass of Paul VI which Lefebvre raises in this letter.The article of P.-M. Gy proved very helpful in the preparation of the final draft of this commentary.

12. The word "normally" indicates that the ordained need not always preach the Gospel in order to fulfill the essential ministry to which they are called in the Mass. *Dominicae Cenae* reflects the viewpoint of the Council of Trent, session xxiii, *Decretum de sacra. ordinis,* canon 1. This canon rejects the following opinions: (1) there is no visible and external priesthood in the New Testament; (2) there exists no power of consecration and offering the true body and blood of Christ; (3) there exists only the office and ministry of preaching the Gospel; (4) those who do not preach are not priests (H. Denzinger and A. Schönmetzer, eds., *Enchiridion Symbolorum, Definitionum et Declarationum de Rebus Fidei et Morum* [DS], 32nd ed. [Freiburg im Br.: Herder, 1963] 1771).

13. Session xxii, *Decretum de Missa,* canon 2 (DS 1752). This canon rejects a separation of the Last Supper from the origins of the sacrament of the priesthood; it affirms the christological grounding of the ordained ministry of the Eucharist; it does not prevent, despite use of the words *institutio* and *ordinatio,* a more precise description of the historical unfolding of ecclesiastical office; it provides an opening for the insertion (into a more comprehensive ministry of preaching the Gospel as is done in Vatican II, *Lumen Gentium,* 25) of the idea of preaching through the Eucharist the death of the Lord.

14. Cf. Council of Trent, session xiv, *Decretum de paenit. et unct. extr.,* canon 3 (DS 1703) and the *Doctrina de sacra. paenitentiae,* ch. 1 (DS 1670); also, *Concilium Tridentinum. Diariorum, Actorum, Epistularum, Tractatuum nova collectio,* ed. Societas Goerresiana (CT), VI/1 (Freiburg im Br.: Herder, 1901ff.) 396.

15. Cf. G. Fahrnberger, *Bischofsamt und Priestertum in den Diskussionen des Konzils von Trient: Eine Rechtstheologische Untersuchung.* Wiener Beiträge zur Theologie 30 (Wien: Herder, 1970) *passim.*

16. Cf. H. Müller, *Zum Verhältnis zwischen Episcopat und Presbyterat in zweiten vaticanischen Konzil: Eine Rechtstheologische Untersuchung.* Wiener Beiträge zur Theologie 35 (Wien: Herder, 1971) *passim.*

17. The lack of clarity is due to the inability of the theologians and Fathers at Trent to choose between one or other of the more precise interpretations of the relation of the Eucharistic action at the Last Supper to the institution of the *ordo sacerdotalis.* The more favored opinion seems to come down to this mode of reasoning: Christ instituted a cultic sacrifice at the Last Supper. *Atqui,* by its very nature, cultic sacrifice requires a cultic priesthood. *Ergo,* implicitly Christ instituted a cultic priesthood. This canon was rejected by several influential Fathers because, as Granada stated, it was not discussed by the theologians and was insufficiently examined by the Fathers (H. Jedin, *Geschichte des Konzils von Trient* IV/1 [Freiburg: Herder, 1975] 207–208).

18. The relevant section of the *doctrina,* ch. 1, reads: "Christ offered himself under the species of bread and wine to God the Father and under the symbols of these same things handed them to the apostles (whom he then constituted priests of the New Testament—*quos tunc novi testamenti sacerdotes constituebat—*) to consume, and by the words 'Do this . . .' he ordered them and their successors in the priesthood to offer, as the Catholic Church has always understood and taught, in order that he might leave a visible sacrifice . . . by which the unbloody sacrifice accomplished on the cross once for all might be represented" (DS 1740). It is noteworthy that in session xxiii of Trent, Bishop Martinus Perezius de Ayala (Spain) observed that it would be contradictory to say that the apostles were ordained by the words *accipite et bibite.* However, the editor of the critical edition of the *Acta,* Ehses, states that this is what is said in ch. 1 of the *doctrina* on the Mass: *Immo plene concordantia cum ibi in doctrina de sacrificio missae, cap. I, statuatur in porrectione specierum panis et vini, id est corpus et sanguis sui, Christum apostolos sacredotes constituisse* (CT IX, 75, n. 2).

19. It seems clear that the memorial command was not understood in the New Testament Church to refer explicitly to the ministry of the Eucharist, let alone the *ordo sacerdotalis.* It receives an interpretation in 1 Corinthians 11:26, "As often as you eat the bread and drink the cup you proclaim the death. . . ." This means, at least, that the eating and drinking is an affirmation of the salvific meaning of the death of Christ. In a good survey and evaluation of recent research on the history of tradition of the New Testament accounts of the institution of the Eucharist, H. Merklein notes that

a completely satisfactory explanation of the memorial command based on exegesis seems unattainable ("Erwägungen zur Überlieferungsgeschichte des neutestamentlichen Abendmahlstraditionen," *Biblische Zeitschrift* 21 [1977] 98–99). But to the extent that this question is not resolved, any precise determination of its original meaning remains problematic.

20. *Dominicae Cenae* refers in n. 3 to the text of the anaphora found in A. Hänggi and I. Pahl, *Prex Eucharistica: Textus et variis liturgiis antiquioribus selecti.* Spicilegium Friburgense 12 (Fribourg: University of Fribourg, 1968) 183. This anaphora prefers the formulation of the account of institution which makes 1 Corinthians 11:26 a word of the Lord! It omits the twice repeated "Do this . . ." of the Pauline tradition (vv. 24b, 25b).

21. Cf. DS 1740, ". . . as the Catholic Church has always understood and taught" (quoted above, n. 18).

22. In a footnote (n. 4), *Dominicae Cenae* refers to the first liturgical evidence for the practice of the newly ordained bishop acting as celebrant of the Eucharist following episcopal consecration. This is found in *Apostolic Tradition* of Hippolytus (B. Botte, ed., *La tradition apostolique de saint Hippolyte.* Liturgiewissenschaftliche Quellen und Forschungen 39 [Münster im Westf.: Aschendorff, ²1963] 5–17, nos. 2–4). The same source does not offer direct evidence for the linking of the celebration of the Eucharist to the ordination of presbyter and deacon (*ibid.,* 21–23, nos. 7–8). But the special relation of the presbyter and deacon to the Eucharist is shown by the fact that presbyters impose hands over the oblation with the newly ordained bishop (no. 4), deacons present the oblation to the bishop (no. 4), and presbyters and deacons have special roles in the distribution of Holy Communion (*ibid.,* 61, no. 22).

23. *Dominicae Cenae* refers this quotation to 1 Peter 2:5 (n. 6). While the letter situates the scriptural text within the prespective of the Eucharistic mystery under all its aspects, 1 Peter refers more specifically to the worship offered to God through the witness of a holy life in the world (cf. 1 Pet. 2:11ff.).

24. Vatican II's *Magna Carta* for the laity, *Lumen Gentium* 30–38, stresses the common responsibility of all members for the mission of the Church, while distinguishing special responsibilities based on particular gifts and calling.

25. Laity have often possessed the special charism to inspire the "healthy Eucharistic piety" of which *Dominicae Cenae* speaks. The role of religious women has been considerable. The telling influence of religious who are priests has frequently been grounded on the orientation of the religious rule and not precisely inspired by their vocation to ordained ministry. The outstanding contribution of Ignatius of Loyola in the middle of the six-

teenth century, which was often opposed by clergy of high rank, was due to inspiration received as a layman.

26. *Sacrosanctum Concilium* 47ff.

27. A title used by the Council of Trent, session xxii: *Decretum de ss. Missae sacrificio.*

28. The *Dialogue with Heraclides* affords third century evidence for the explicit reflection on the question of the addressees of the Eucharistic Prayer. The problem was this: To whom should the *prosphora* (= Eucharistic Prayer) be directed: to the Father or Son? What is the role of the Son in the offering? Origen answers that "the *prosphora* is made always to the all-powerful God by the intermediary of Jesus Christ, insofar as he communicates with the Father by his divinity; the *prosphora* is not made in two ways, but to God by the intermediary of God" (J. Scherer, ed., *Entretien d'Origene avec Heraclides.* Sources chrétiennes 67 [Paris: Cerf, 1960] 63). Origen's failure to take account of the human mediation of Jesus Christ in the Eucharist is typical of the early Alexandrian neglect of the role of the humanity of Jesus in the work of salvation. But he does witness to the liturgical tradition of his time in the matter of the primary addressee of the Eucharistic Prayer.

29. Cf. J. A. Jungmann, *Die Stellung Christi im liturgischen Gebet* (Münster im Westf.: Aschendorff, 1925); Eng. tr., *The Place of Christ in Liturgical Prayer* (Staten Island, N.Y.: Alba, 1965).

30. Cf. B. Fischer, "Le Christ dans les Psalmes," *La Maison-Dieu* 27 (1951) 86–113.

31. *Sacrosanctum Concilium* 7.2.

32. *Dominicae Cenae* 3.1 describes the words "This is my body given for you . . ." as spoken at the moment of "supreme dedication and total abandonment of himself." Thus it points to an offering made by Christ of himself at the Last Supper. The nature of the offering is explained further in chapters 4, 8, and 9.

33. *Dominicae Cenae* stresses that the Eucharist is a sacramental celebration of the whole mystery of Christ, including the death and resurrection. Thus it conforms to patristic theology and the liturgical tradition of the united Church of the first millennium which viewed the death of Christ as linked inexorably to the resurrection, and the celebration of the Eucharist as the re-presentation of the *transitus ad gloriam per mortem* into which the community is drawn.

34. The Vulgate translation of this verse uses the phrase *semet ipsum exinanivit* to refer to the divesting of the status of glory to which the divine Son had a right. *Dominicae Cenae,* however, employs the noun *exinanitio* to refer to Christ's death.

35. In n. 13 the observation is made that "the value of this cult and the power of sanctification of these forms of piety in the Eucharist do not depend on the forms themselves but on the interior attitude of the mind." Thus a distinction is made between them and participation in the Mass and the reception of the Eucharistic species. In classical Scholastic theology the distinction is made between the effect *ex opere operato* and *ex opere operantis.* The former term is applied to the Mass as act of Christ and to the reception of Holy Communion. To what extent this viewpoint is suggested by *Dominicae Cenae* is not clear.

36. "Reparation" is not equated with the Eucharistic cult but seen as a consequence of it. From other passages of *Dominicae Cenae* it seems clear that acts of reparation should take the form of social works of love (cf. ch. 6.2).

37. This formula of H. de Lubac, *Meditation sur l'église* (Paris: ²1953) 129–137, directly inspired Vatican II's *Lumen Gentium* 26.1, which speaks of the Eucharist, *under the care of the bishop,* as a means by which "the Church continually lives and grows." *Dominicae Cenae* refers in n. 16 to *Lumen Gentium* 11, where the role of the Eucharist in the life of the whole Church is explained, and to the apparatus of the preparatory schemas in which de Lubac's formula and supporting references from tradition are found. In this way it places in relief the more general meaning of the formula which is not confined merely to the bishop's particular role.

38. This formula is found in *Lumen Gentium* 11.1.

39. The Council of Trent, session xiii, *Decretum de ss. eucharistia,* ch. 3 of the *doctrina,* states that "before the apostles received the Eucharist from the hand of the Lord, he affirmed it to be his body and blood and the Church has always believed that after the consecration the true body of the Lord and the true blood of the Lord exist (*exsistere*) under the species of bread and wine together with his soul and divinity" (DS 1640). The relationship between the offering of Christ at the Last Supper and the cross and Eucharistic sacrifice is discussed in chapter 8 of *Dominicae Cenae.*

40. In chapter 11.2 of *Dominicae Cenae* it is also seen as the birthplace "in a sense" of the collegial unity of the episcopate. The "sense" is not explained.

41. E. J. Kilmartin, "The Eucharist: Nourishment for Communion," in G. D' Ercole, ed., *Populus Dei II: Ecclesia.* Communio 11 (Rome: Christen, 1969) 1067–1072.

42. S. Tromp, "De nativitate Ecclesiae ex corde Jesu in Cruce," *Gregorianum* 13 (1932) 489–529; *idem,* ed., *Pius Papa XII: De Mysterio Jesu Christi Corpore.* Texte et Documenta: series theologicae 26 (Rome: Gregor-

ianum, 1948) 93–96: citation of supporting patristic testimony to the passage of the encyclical letter *Mystici Corporis* 27, 2–4, which affirms that the Church was born from the side of Christ.

43. Cf. above, n. 18.

44. DS 1752.

45. DS 1751.

46. DS 1740 and 1742.

47. DS 1753.

48. DS 1754.

49. H. Jedin, *op. cit.*, 174–209; F. Pratzner, *Messe und Kreuzesopfer: Die Krise der sakramentalen Idee bei Luther und der mittelalterlichen Scholastik.* Weiner Beiträge zur Theologie 29 (Wien: Herder, 1970) 27–52.

50 "With greater certainty" recalls the teaching of the Council of Trent, *Decretum de sacramentis,* canon 8, ". . . through the sacrament of the New Law grace is conferred *ex opere operato*" (DS 1608), and canon 7, ". . . on the side of God, grace is given through . . . the sacraments always and to all" (DS 1607) The expression "with greater . . . power" recalls the outmoded Scholastic theory that, *caeteris paribus,* sacraments bestow more grace than do "non-sacramental" means of sanctification. As employed in *Dominicae Cenae* the latter expression could refer to the special character of the sacraments as acts of the Church which address the recipients in their individuality (E. J. Kilmartin, "A Modern Approach to the Word of God and Sacraments of Christ: Perspectives and Principles," in F. Eigo, ed., *The Sacraments: God's Love and Mercy Actualized.* Proceedings of the Theological Institute of Villanova University [Villanova: University Press, 1979] 93–94).

51. Here *Dominicae Cenae* touches on a topic that has received little comment in Catholic theology and liturgical studies except for general statements about the ideal Eucharist. More serious attention needs to be paid to the way in which the liturgy is celebrated so that it may contribute to the transformation of society. The mode of celebration can, for example, be the instrument of oppressive structures (E. J. Kilmartin, "A Modern Approach," 94–96).

52. F. Pratzner, *op. cit.;* Th. Schneider, "Opfer Jesu Christi und der Kirche zum Verständnis der Aussagen des Konzils von Trient," *Catholica* 41 (1977) 51–65.

53. L. Scheffczyk reviews the literature on this question in "Die Zuordnung von Sakrament und Opfer in der Eucharistie," Faculty of the University of Munich, ed., *Pro Mundi Vita* (Munich: Kosel, 1960) 203–222.

54. CT VIII, 768.

55. F. Pratzner, *op. cit.*, 52.

56. For a good discussion of the relation of the Eucharist to the historical Jesus see H. Patsch, *Abendmahl und historischer Jesus* (Stuttgart: Caliver, 1972); also H. Merklein, *op. cit.,* 238.

57. *The General Instruction of the Roman Mass,* nos. 6–9, in *Selected Documents from the New Sacramentary* (Washington, D.C.: USCC, 1974) 23–24.

58. Apart from the Barberini Gr. 366 (Vatican Apostolic Library, fol. 8, 17–20), this reading is found in F. Renaudot, *Liturgiam orientalium collecta* I (Freiburg a.M.: ²1847).

59. For a brief, accurate description of the history and interpretation of Barberini Gr. 366, see R. Taft, *The Great Entrance: A History of the Transfer of Gifts and Other Pre-Anaphoral Rites of the Liturgy of St. John Chrysostom. Orientalia Christiana Analecta* 200 (Rome: PISO, 1975) 136–138.

60. See E. J. Kilmartin, *Toward Reunion,* 35–52, for a discussion of the recently constituted International Orthodox-Roman Catholic Dialogue.

61. R. Hotz, *Sakramente—im Wechselspiel zwischen Ost und West. Ökumenische Theologie* 2 (Zürich: Benziger, 1979) 235–241, presents a good summary of the main objections of modern Orthodox theologians to Vatican II's interpretation of the relationship of priest to Christ in the celebration of the Eucharist. Within Orthodox pneumatology and ecclesiology the priest is understood to act *in nomine ecclesiae* and so *in persona Christi.*

62. For a brief description of the circumstances of this rupture and its significance, see E. J. Kilmartin, *Toward Reunion,* 8–9.

63. *Dominicae Cenae* refers to *The General Instruction,* no. 49 c (*op. cit.,* 38) which speaks of the "rite of carrying up the gifts."

64. *The General Instruction,* no. 55 f (*op. cit.,* 39).

65. *The General Instruction,* no. 49 d (*op. cit.,* 38) links the offertory collection to the presentation of gifts. Moreover in the apostolic letter *Firma in Traditione,* June 15, 1974, Paul VI relates the Mass stipend to the old offertory procession. It is viewed as a means by which the faithful more intimately associate themselves with the Eucharistic sacrifice (A. Flannery ed., *Vatican Council II: The Conciliar and Post-Conciliar Docements* [Collegeville: Liturgical Press, 1975] 277).

66. This prayer offers a point of contact with the Orthodox theology of Eucharistic Communion. In keeping with the Greek patristic tradition, Orthodox theologians affirm that Communion of the body and blood of Christ is a symbolic expression of communion of the Holy Spirit.

67. Ch. 9.6; n. 50 (DS 1740).

68. The weakness of the argument of ch. 1 of the *doctrina* (DS 1739–1742) was noted by Bishop Antonius Justinianus, O.F.M., in the General Congregation of August 6, 1562, *Doctrina non placet, quia procedimus ex*

principiis debilibus, cum illos tres auctoritates adductum: Melchisedek, Malachi et Evangelium, cum potius haec habemus per traditionem (CT VIII, 756).

69. DS 1743.

70. *Dei Verbum*, 21.

71. *Presbyterorum Ordinis*, 18.

72. *Sacrosanctum Concilium*, 48 and 51.

73. *Mensa enim domini ... mensa lectionum dominicarum*, in Hilary of Poitiers, *Tractatus in Ps* 127.10 (Corpus Scriptorum Ecclesiasticorum Latinorum XXII [Vienna, 1891] 635).

74. *Ser. in Matt* 85 (Griechische Christliche Schriftsteller der ersten drei Jahrhunderte 41 [Leipzig, 1941] 196); *Comm. in John* 32.24 (GCS 10 [Leipzig, 1903] 468.

75. *Hom. in Num* 16.9 (GCS 30 [Leipzig, 1921] 152).

76. *Sacrosanctum Concilium*, 7.

77. AAS 57 (1965) 762–764.

78. *Hom. in Exod* 13.3 (GCS 29 [Leipzig, 1920] 264).

79. L. Lies, *Wort und Eucharistie bei Origenes: Zur Spiritualisierungstendenz des Eucharistieverständnis*. Innsbrucker theologische Studien I (Innsbruck: Tyrolia, 1978).

80. P.-M. Gy, *op. cit.*, 25.

81. *Dei Verbum* 21.1.

82. Ep. 37.2 (A. Thiel, *Epistulae Romanorum Pontificum ... a S. Hilario usque ad Pelagium II*, I (Brunsberg: 1868).

83. J. P. De Jong, *L'Eucharistie comme realité symbolique* (Paris: Cerf, 1972) 111–119.

84. DS 1198. R. Damerau, *Der Laienkelch*. Studien zu den Grundlagen der Reformation II (Giessen: W. Schmitz, 1964), offers a good contribution to the proper understanding of the motives and arguments which supported the position of the Council of Constance.

85. Cf. *Dominicae Cenae* 7.5.

86. *Lumen Gentium* 11.1.

87. *Unitatis Redintegratio* 15.3; *Orientalium Ecclesiarum* 27–29.

88. *Dominicae Cenae*, nn. 68–69.

89. Cf. *On Admitting Other Christians to Eucharistic Communion in the Catholic Church* (AAS 64 [1972] 518–525) and the interpretation of this instruction (AAS 65 [1973] 616–619).

90. DS 812.

91. *S.T. Supplementum* q. 6, art. 3, ad 3.

92. E.g., St. Bonaventure, *In IV Sent.* dist. 17, art. 4, q. 1.

93. E.g., St. Thomas, *In IV Sent.* dist. 12, q. 3, art. 1, q. 2.

94. E.g., St. John of the Cross, Lib. 1 *Noctis obscurae,* ch. 6.

95. DS 3375–3383.

96. C.I.C., canon 1367, par. 2, states that seminarians should confess at least twice a week and frequently receive Holy Communion.

97. *Lumen Gentium* 11.

98. AAS 61 (1968) 806.

99. E. J. Kilmartin, "The One Fruit and the Many Fruits of the Mass," *Proceedings of the Catholic Theological Society of America* 21 (1966) 57–64.

100. For a recent discussion of the relevance of the relationship of the question of the role of the universal Church to the theology of Mass stipend proposed by Paul VI in *Firma in Traditione,* see E. J. Kilmartin, "Money and the Ministry of the Sacraments," in W. Bassett and P. Huizing, eds., *The Finances of the Church.* Concilium 117 (New York: Seabury, 1979) 104–111.

101. Lib. 2, cap. 13 (J. P. Migne, ed., *Patrologiae Cursus Completus, Series Latina* CV [Paris: 1864] 1088); (PL).

102. J. D. Mansi, ed., *Sacrorum Conciliorum nova collectio* XV (Paris and Leipzig: Welter, 1902) 882.

103. M. Andrieu, *Le Pontifical Romain au Moyen-Age. I: Le Pontifical Romain du XII siècle.* Studi e Testi 86 (Vatican City, 1938).

104. Sermo 3 (PL 162 [Paris: 1889] 526).

Appendix

The Text of *Dominicae Cenae:*
The Mystery and Worship
of the Holy Eucharist

My venerable and dear brothers,

1. Again this year, for Holy Thursday, I am writing a letter to all of you. This letter has an immediate connection with the one which you received last year on the same occasion, together with the letter to the priests. I wish in the first place to thank you cordially for having accepted my previous letters with that spirit of unity which the Lord established between us, and also for having transmitted to your priests the thoughts that I desired to express at the beginning of my pontificate.

During the Eucharistic liturgy of Holy Thursday, you renewed, together with your priests, the promises and commitments undertaken at the moment of ordination. Many of you, venerable and dear brothers, told me about it later, also adding words of personal thanks, and indeed often sending those expressed by your priests. Furthermore, many priests expressed their joy, both because of the profound and solemn character of Holy Thursday as the annual "feast of priests" and also because of the importance of the subjects dealt with in the letter addressed to them.

Those replies form a rich collection which once more indicates how dear to the vast majority of priests of the Catholic Church is the path of the priestly life, the path along which this Church has been journeying for centuries: how much they love and esteem it, and how much they desire to follow it for the future.

At this point I must add that only a certain number of matters were dealt with in the letter to priests, as was in fact emphasized at the beginning of the document.[1] Furthermore, the main stress was laid upon the pastoral character of the priestly ministry but this certainly does not mean that those groups of priests who are not engaged in direct pastoral activity were not also taken into consideration. In this regard I would refer once more to the teaching of the Second Vatican Council, and also to the declarations of the 1971 Synod of Bishops.

The pastoral character of the priestly ministry does not cease to mark the life of every priest, even if the daily tasks that he carries out are not explicitly directed to the pastoral administration of the sacraments. In this sense, the letter written to the priests on Holy Thursday was addressed to them all, without any exception, even though, as I said above, it did not deal with all the aspects of the life and activity of priests. I think this clarification is useful and opportune at the beginning of the present letter.

I. The Eucharistic Mystery in the Life of the Church and of the Priest

Eucharist and Priesthood

2. The present letter that I am addressing to you, my venerable and dear brothers in the episcopate—and which is, as I have said, in a certain way a continuation of the previous one—is also closely linked with the mystery of Holy Thursday, and is related to the priesthood. In fact I intend to devote it to the Eucharist, and in particular to certain aspects of the Eucharistic mystery and its impact on the lives of those who are the ministers of it; and so those to whom this letter is directly addressed are you, the bishops of the Church; together with you, all the priests, and, in their own rank, the deacons too.

In reality, the ministerial and hierarchical priesthood, the priesthood of the bishops and the priests, and, at their side, the ministry of the deacons—ministries which normally begin with the proclamation of the Gospel—are in the closest relationship with the Eucharist. The Eucharist is the principal and central *raison d'être* of the sacrament of the priesthood, which effectively came into being at the moment of the institution of the Eucharist, and together with it.[2] Not without reason the words "Do this in memory of me" are said immediately after the words of Eucharistic consecration, and we repeat them every time we celebrate the holy sacrifice.[3]

Through our ordination—the celebration of which is linked to the holy Mass from the very first liturgical evidence[4]—we are united in a singular and exceptional way to the Eucharist. In a certain way we derive from it and exist for it. We are also, and in a special way, responsible for it—each priest in his own community and each bishop by virtue of the care of all the communities entrusted to him, on the basis of the *sollicitudo omnium ecclesiarum* that St. Paul speaks of.[5] Thus we bishops and priests are entrusted with the great "mystery of faith," and while it is also given to the whole people of God, to all believers in Christ, yet to us has been entrusted the Eucharist also "for" others, who expect from us a particular witness of veneration and love toward this sacrament, so that they too may be able to be built up and vivified "to offer spiritual sacrifices."[6]

In this way our Eucharistic worship, both in the celebration of Mass and in our devotion to the blessed sacrament, is like a life-giving current that links our ministerial or hierarchical priesthood to the common priesthood of the faithful, and presents it in its vertical dimension and with its central value. The priest fulfills his principal mission and is manifested in all his fullness when he celebrates the Eucharist,[7] and this manifestation is more complete when he himself allows the depth of that mystery to become visible, so that it alone shines forth in people's hearts and minds through his ministry. This is the supreme exercise of the "kingly priesthood," "the source and summit of all Christian life."[8]

Worship of the Eucharistic Mystery

3. This worship is directed toward God the Father through Jesus Christ in the Holy Spirit. In the first place it is directed toward the Father, who, as St. John's Gospel says, "loved the world so much that he gave his only Son, so that everyone who believes in him may not be lost but may have eternal life."[9]

It is also directed, in the Holy Spirit, to the incarnate Son, in the economy of salvation, especially at that moment of supreme dedication and total abandonment of himself to which the words uttered in the Upper Room refer: "This is my body given up for you. . . . This is the cup of my blood shed for you."[10] The liturgical acclamation "We proclaim your death, Lord Jesus" takes us back precisely to that moment; and with the proclamation of his resurrection we embrace in the same act of veneration Christ risen and glorified "at the right hand of the Father," as also the expectation of his "coming in glory." Yet it is the voluntary annihilation, accepted by the Father and glorified with the resurrection, which, sacramentally celebrated together with the resurrection, brings us to adore the Redeemer who "became obedient unto death, even death on a cross."[11]

And this adoration of ours contains yet another special characteristic. It is compenetrated by the greatness of that human death, in whch the world, that is to say, each one of us, has been loved "to the end."[12] Thus it is also a response that tries to repay that love immolated even to the death on the cross: It is our "Eucharist," that is to say, our giving him thanks, our praise of him for having redeemed us by his death and made us sharers in immortal life through his resurrection.

This worship, given therefore to the Trinity of the Father and of the Son and of the Holy Spirit, above all accompanies and permeates the celebration of the Eucharistic liturgy. But it must fill our churches also outside the timetable of Masses. Indeed, since the Eucharistic mystery was instituted out of love and makes Christ sacramentally present, it is worthy of thanksgiving and worship. And this worship must be prominent in all our encounters with the blessed sacrament, both whcn we visit our churches and when the sacred species are taken to the sick and administered to them.

Adoration of Christ in this sacrament of love must also find expression in various forms of Eucharistic devotion: personal prayer before the blessed sacrament, hours of adoration, periods of exposition—short, prolonged and annual (Forty Hours)—Eucharistic benediction, Eucharistic processions, Eucharistic congresses.[13] A particular mention should be made at this point of the solemnity of the body and blood of Christ as an act of public worship rendered to Christ present in the Eucharist, a feast instituted by my predecessor Urban IV in memory of the institution of this great mystery.[14] All this therefore corresponds to the general principles and particular norms already long in existence but newly formulated during or after the Second Vatican Council.[15]

The encouragement and the deepening of Eucharistic worship are proofs of that authentic renewal which the Council set itself as an aim and of which they are the central point. And this, venerable and dear brothers, deserves separate reflection. The Church and the world have a great need of Eucharistic worship. Jesus waits for us in this sacrament of love. Let us be generous with our time in going to meet him in adoration and in contemplation that is full of faith and ready to make reparation for the great faults and crimes of the world. May our adoration never cease.

Eucharist and Church

4. Thanks to the Council we have realized with renewed force the following truth: Just as the Church "makes the Eucharist," so "the Eucharist builds up" the Church;[16] and this truth is closely bound up with the mystery of Holy Thursday. The Church was founded, as the new community of the people of God, in the apostolic community of those twelve who, at the Last Supper, became partakers of the body and blood of the Lord under the species of bread and wine. Christ had said to them: "Take and eat. . . . Take and drink." And carrying out this command of his, they entered for the first time into sacramental communion with the Son of God, a communion that is a pledge of eternal life. From that moment until the end of time, the Church is being built up through that same communion with the Son of God, a communion which is a pledge of the eternal Passover.

Dear and venerable brothers in the episcopate, as teachers and custodians of the salvific truth of the Eucharist, we must always and everywhere preserve this meaning and this dimension of the sacramental encounter and intimacy with Christ. It is precisely these elements which constitute the very substance of Eucharistic worship.

The meaning of the truth expounded above in no way diminishes—in fact it facilitates—the Eucharistic character of spiritual drawing together and union between the people who share in the sacrifice, which then in Communion becomes for them the banquet. This drawing together and this union, the prototype of which is the union of the apostles about Christ at the Last Supper, express the Church and bring her into being.

But the Church is not brought into being only through the union of people, through the experience of brotherhood to which the Eucharistic banquet gives rise. The Church is brought into being when, in that fraternal union and communion, we celebrate the sacrifice of the cross of Christ, when we proclaim "the Lord's death until he comes,"[17] and later, when, being deeply compenetrated with the mystery of our salvation, we approach as a community the table of the Lord, in order to be nourished there, in a sacramental manner, by the fruits of the holy sacrifice of propitiation. Therefore in Eucharistic Communion we receive Christ, Christ himself; and our union with him, which is a gift and grace for each individual, brings it about that in him we are also associated in the unity of his body which is the Church.

Only in this way, through that faith and that disposition of mind, is there brought about that building up of the Church, which in the Eucharist truly finds its "source and summit," according to the well-known expression of the Second Vatican Council.[18] This truth, which as a result of the same Council has received a new and vigorous emphasis,[19] must be a frequent theme of our reflection and teaching. Let all pastoral activity be nourished by it, and may it also be food for ourselves and for all the priests who collaborated with us, and likewise for the whole of the communities entrusted to us. In this practice there should thus be revealed, almost at every step, that close relationship between the Church's spiritual and apostolic vitality and the Eucharist, understood in the profound significance and from all points of view.[20]

Eucharist and Charity

5. Before proceeding to more detailed observations on the subject of the celebration of the holy sacrifice, I wish briefly to reaffirm the fact that Eucharistic worship constitutes the soul of all Christian life. In fact Christian life is expressed in the fulfilling of the greatest commandment, that is to say, in the love of God and neighbor, and this love finds its source in the blessed sacrament which is commonly called the sacrament of love.

The Eucharist signifies this charity, and therefore recalls it, makes it present and at the same time brings it about. Every time that we consciously share in it, there opens in our souls a real dimension of that unfathomable love that includes everything that God has done and continues to do for us human beings, as Christ says: "My Father goes on working, and so do I."[21] Together with this unfathomable and free gift, which is charity revealed in its fullest degree in the saving sacrifice of the Son of God, the sacrifice of which the Eucharist is the indelible sign, there also springs up within us a lively response of love.We not only know love; we ourselves begin to love. We enter, so to speak, upon the path of love and along this path make progress. Thanks to the Eucharist, the love that springs up within us from the Eucharist develops in us, becomes deeper and grows stronger.

Eucharistic worship is therefore precisely the expression of that love which is the authentic and deepest characteristic of the Christian vocation. This worship springs from the love and serves the love to which we are all called in Jesus Christ.[22] A living fruit of this worship is the perfecting of the image of God that we bear within us, an image that corresponds to the one that Christ has revealed to us. As we thus become adorers of the Father "in spirit and truth,"[23] we mature in an ever fuller union with Christ, we are ever more united to him, and—if one may use the expression—we are ever more in harmony with him.

The doctrine of the Eucharist, the sign of unity and bond of charity, taught by St. Paul,[24] has been in subsequent times deepened by the writings of very many saints who are a living example for us of Eucharistic worship. We must always have this reality before our eyes, and at the same time we must continually try to bring it about that our own generation too may add new examples to those marvelous examples of the past, new examples no less living and eloquent, that will reflect the age to which we belong.

Eucharist and Neighbor

6. The authentic sense of the Eucharist becomes of itself the school of active love for neighbor. We know that this is the true and full order of love that the Lord has taught us: "By this love you have for one another, everyone will know that you are my disciples."[25] The Eucharist educates us to this love in a deeper way; it shows us, in fact, what values each person, our brother or sister, has in God's eyes, if Christ offers himself equally to each one, under the species of bread and wine. If our Eucharistic worship is authentic, it must make us grow in awareness of the dignity of each person. The awareness of that dignity becomes the deepest motive of our relationship with our neighbor.

We must also become particularly sensitive to all human suffering and misery, to all injustice and wrong, and seek the way to redress them effectively. Let us learn to discover with respect the truth about the inner self of people, for it is precisely this inner self that becomes the dwelling place of God present in the Eucharist. Christ comes into the hearts of our brothers and sisters and visits their consciences. How the image of each and every one changes, when we become aware of this reality, when we make it the subject of our reflections! The sense of the Eucharistic mystery leads us to a love for our neighbor, to a love for every human being.[26]

Eucharist and Life

7. Since therefore the Eucharist is the source of charity, it has always been at the center of the life of Christ's disciples. It has the appearance of bread and wine, that is to say, of food and drink; it is therefore as familiar to people, as closely linked to their life as food and drink. The veneration of God, who is love, springs, in Eucharistic worship, from that kind of intimacy in which he himself, by analogy with food and drink, fills our spiritual being, ensuring its life, as food and drink do. This "Eucharistic" veneration of God therefore strictly corresponds to his saving plan. He himself, the Father, wants the "true worshipers"[27] to worship him precisely in this way, and it is Christ who expresses this desire, both with his words and likewise with this sacrament in which he makes possible worship of the Father in the way most in conformity with the Father's will.

From this concept of Eucharistic worship there then stems the whole sacramental style of the Christian's life. In fact, leading a life based on the sacraments and animated by the common priesthood means in the first place that Christians desire God to act in them in order to enable them to attain, in the Spirit, "the fullness of Christ himself."[28] God, on his part, does not touch them only through events and by this inner grace; he also acts in them with greater certainty and power through the sacraments. The sacraments give the lives of Christians a sacramental style.

Now, of all the sacraments, it is the Holy Eucharist that brings to fullness their initiation as Christians and confers upon the exercise of the common priesthood that sacramental and ecclesial form that links it—as we mentioned before[29]—to the exercise of the ministerial priesthood. In this way Eucharistic worship is the center and goal of all sacramental life.[30] In the depths of Eucharistic worship we find a continual echo of the sacraments of Christian initiation: baptism and confirmation. Where better is there expressed the truth that we are not only "called God's children" but "that is what we are"[31] by virtue of the sacrament of baptism, if not precisely in the fact that in the Eucharist we become partakers of the body and blood of God's only Son? And what predisposes us more to be "true witnesses of Christ"[32] before the world—as we are enabled to be by the sacrament of confirmation—than Eucharistic Communion, in which Christ bears witness to us, and we to him?

It is impossible to analyze here in greater detail the links between the Eucharist and the other sacraments, in particular with the sacrament of family life and the sacrament of the sick. In the encyclical *Redemptor Hominis*[33] I have already drawn attention to the close link between the sacrament of penance and the sacrament of the Eucharist. It is not only that penance leads to the Eucharist, but that the Eucharist also leads to penance. For when we realize who it is that we receive in Eucharistic Communion, there springs up in us almost spontaneously a sense of unworthiness, together with sorrow for our sins and an interior need for purification.

But we must always take care that this great meeting with Christ in the Eucharist does not become a mere habit, and that we do not receive him unworthily, that is to say, in a state of mortal sin.

The practice of the virtue of penance and the sacrament of penance are essential for sustaining in us and continually deepening that spirit of veneration which man owes to God himself and to his love so marvelously revealed.

The purpose of these words is to put forward some general reflections on worship of the Eucharistic mystery, and they could be developed at greater length and more fully. In particular, it would be possible to link what has been said about the effects of the Eucharist on love for others with what we have just noted about commitments undertaken toward humanity and the Church in Eucharistic Communion, and then outline the picture of that "new earth"[34] that springs from the Eucharist through every "new self."[35] In this sacrament of bread and wine, of food and drink, everything that is human really undergoes a singular transformation and elevation. Eucharistic worship is not so much worship of the inaccessible transcendence as worship of the divine condescension, and it is also the merciful and redeeming transformation of the world in the human heart.

Recalling all this only very briefly, I wish, notwithstanding this brevity, to create a wider context for the questions that I shall subsequently have to deal with. These questions are closely linked with the celebration of the holy sacrifice. In fact, in that celebration there is expressed in a more direct way the worship of the Eucharist. This worship comes from the heart, as a most precious homage inspired by the faith, hope and charity that were infused into us at baptism. And it is precisely about this that I wish to write to you in this letter, venerable and dear brothers in the episcopate, and with you to the priests and deacons. It will be followed by detailed indications from the Sacred Congregation for the Sacraments and Divine Worship.

II. The Sacred Character
of the Eucharist and Sacrifice

Sacred Character

8. Beginning with the Upper Room and Holy Thursday, the celebration of the Eucharist has a long history, a history as long as that of the Church. In the course of this history the secondary elements have undergone certain changes, but there has been no change in the essence of the *mysterium* instituted by the Redeemer of the world at the Last Supper. The Second Vatican Council too brought alterations, as a result of which the present liturgy of the Mass is different in some ways from the one known before the Council. We do not intend to speak of these differences. It is better that we should now concentrate on what is essential and immutable in the Eucharistic liturgy.

There is a close link between this element of the Eucharist and its sacredness, that is to say, its being a holy and sacred action. That action is holy and sacred because in it are the continual presence and action of Christ, "the Holy One" of God,[36] "anointed with the Holy Spirit,"[37] "consecrated by the Father"[38] to lay down his life of his own accord and to take it up again,[39] and the High Priest of the new covenant.[40] For it is he who, represented by the celebrant, makes his entrance into the sanctuary and proclaims his Gospel. It is he who is "the offerer and the offered, the consecrator and the consecrated."[41] The Eucharist is a holy and sacred action, because it constitutes the sacred species, the *sancta sanctis,* that is to say, the "holy things (Christ, the Holy One) given to the holy," as all the Eastern liturgies sing at the moment when the Eucharistic bread is raised in order to invite the faithful to the Lord's Supper.

The sacredness of the Mass, therefore, is not a "sacralization," that is to say, something that man adds to Christ's action in the Upper Room, for the Holy Thursday supper was a sacred rite, a primary and constitutive liturgy, through which Christ, by pledging to give his life for us, himself celebrated sacramentally the mystery of his passion and resurrection, the heart of every Mass. Our Masses, being derived from this liturgy, possess of themselves a complete liturgical form, which, in spite of its variations in line with the families of rites, remains substantially the same. The sacred character of the Mass is a sacredness instituted by Christ. The words and action of every priest, answered by the conscious active participation of the whole Eucharistic assembly, echo the words and action of Holy Thursday.

The priest offers the holy sacrifice *in persona Christi*; this means more than offering "in the name of" or "in the place of" Christ. *In persona* means in specific sacramental identification with "the eternal High Priest"[42] who is the author and principal subject of this sacrifice of his, a sacrifice in which, in truth, nobody can take his place. Only he—only Christ—was able and is always able to be the true and effective "expiation for our sins and . . . for the sins of the whole world."[43] Only his sacrifice—and no one else's—was able and is able to have a "propitiatory power" before God, the Trinity and the Transcendent Holiness. Awareness of this reality throws a certain light on the character and significance of the priest celebrant who, by confecting the holy sacrifice and acting *in persona Christi,* is sacramentally (and ineffably) brought into that most profound sacredness and made part of it, spiritually linking with it in turn all those participating in the Eucharistic assembly.

This sacred rite, which is actuated in different liturgical forms, may lack some secondary elements, but it can in no way lack its essential sacred character and sacramentality, since these are willed by Christ and transmitted and regulated by the Church. Neither can this sacred rite be utilized for other ends. If separated from its distinctive sacrificial and sacramental nature, the Eucharistic mystery simply ceases to be. It admits of no "profane" imitation, an imitation that would very easily (indeed regularly) become a profanation. This must always be remembered, perhaps above all in our time, when we see a tendency to do away with the distinction between the "sacred" and "profane," given the widespread tendency, at least in some places, to desacralize everything.

In view of this fact, the Church has a special duty to safeguard and strengthen the sacredness of the Eucharist. In our pluralistic and often deliberately secularized society, the living faith of the Christian community—a faith always aware of its rights vis-à-vis those who do not share that faith—ensures respect for this sacredness. The duty to respect each person's faith is the complement of the natural and civil right to freedom of conscience and of religion.

The sacred character of the Eucharist has found and continues to find expression in the terminology of theology and the liturgy.[44] This sense of the objective sacred character of the Eucharistic mystery is so much part of the faith of the people of God that their faith is enriched and strengthened by it.[45] Therefore the ministers of the

Eucharist must, especially today, be illumined by the fullness of this living faith, and in its light they must understand and perform all that is part, by Christ's will and the will of his Church, of their priestly ministry.

Sacrifice

9. The Eucharist is above all else a sacrifice. It is the sacrifice of the redemption and also the sacrifice of the new covenant,[46] as we believe and as the Eastern churches clearly profess. "Today's sacrifice," the Greek church stated centuries ago, "is like that offered once by the Only-Begotten Incarnate Word; it is offered by him (now as then), since it is one and the same sacrifice."[47] Accordingly, precisely by making this single sacrifice of our salvation present, man and the world are restored to God through the paschal newness of redemption. This restoration cannot cease to be. It is the foundation of the "new and eternal covenant" of God with man and of man with God. If it were missing, one would have to question both the excellence of the sacrifice of the redemption, which in fact was perfect and definitive, and also the sacrificial value of the Mass. In fact, the Eucharist, being a true sacrifice, brings about this restoration to God.

Consequently, the celebrant, as minister of this sacrifice, is the authentic priest, performing—in virtue of the specific power of sacred ordination—a true sacrificial act that brings creation back to God. Although all those who participate in the Eucharist do not confect the sacrifice as he does, they offer with him, by virtue of the common priesthood, their own spiritual sacrifices represented by the bread and wine from the moment of their presentation at the altar. For this liturgical action, which takes a solemn form in almost all liturgies, has a "spiritual value and meaning."[48] The bread and wine become in a sense a symbol of all that the Eucharistic assembly brings, on its own part, as an offering to God and offers spiritually.

It is important that this first moment of the liturgy of the Eucharist in the strict sense should find expression in the attitude of the participants. There is a link between this and the offertory "procession" provided for in the recent liturgical reform[49] and accompanied, in keeping with ancient tradition, by a psalm or song. A certain length of time must be allowed, so that all can become aware of this act, which is given expression at the same time by the words of the celebrant.

Awareness of the act of presenting the offerings should be maintained throughout the Mass. Indeed, it should be brought to fullness at the moment of the consecration and of the *anamnesis* offering, as is demanded by the fundamental value of the moment of the sacrifice. This is shown by the words of the Eucharistic Prayer said aloud by the priest. It seems worthwhile repeating here some expressions in the third Eucharistic Prayer that show in particular the sacrificial character of the Eucharist and link the offering of our persons with Christ's offering: "Look with favor on your Church's offering, and see the Victim whose death has reconciled us to yourself. Grant that we, who are nourished by his body and blood, may be filled with his Holy Spirit, and become one body, one spirit in Christ. May he make us an everlasting gift to you."

This sacrificial value is expressed earlier in every celebration by the words with which the priest concludes the presentation of the gifts, asking the faithful to pray "that my sacrifice and yours may be acceptable to God, the almighty Father." These words are binding, since they express the character of the entire Eucharistic liturgy and the fullness of its divine and ecclesial content.

All who participate with faith in the Eucharist become aware that it is a "sacrifice," that is to say, a "consecrated offering." For the bread and wine presented at the altar and accompanied by the devotion and the spiritual sacrifices of the participants are finally consecrated, so as to become truly, really and substantially Christ's own body that is given up and his blood that is shed. Thus, by virtue of the consecration, the species of bread and wine re-present[50] in a sacramental unbloody manner the bloody propitiatory sacrifice offered by him on the cross to his Father for the salvation of the world. Indeed, he alone, giving himself as a propitiatory victim in an act of supreme surrender and immolation, has reconciled humanity with the Father, solely through his sacrifice, "having cancelled the bond which stood against us."[51]

To this sacrifice, which is renewed in a sacramental form on the altar, the offerings of bread and wine, united with the devotion of the faithful, nevertheless bring their unique contribution, since by means of the consecration by the priest they become the sacred species. This is made clear by the way in which the priest acts during the Eucharistic Prayer, especially at the consecration, and when the celebration of the holy sacrifice and participation in it are accompanied by awareness that "the Teacher is here and is calling for you."[52] This call of the Lord to us through his sacrifice opens our hearts, so that, purified in the mystery of our redemption, they may be united to him in Eucharistic Communion, which confers upon participation at Mass a value that is mature, complete and binding on human life: "The Church's intention is that the faithful not only offer the spotless Victim but also learn to offer themselves and daily to be drawn into ever more perfect union, through Christ the Mediator, with the Father and with each other, so that at last God may be all in all."[53]

It is therefore very opportune and necessary to continue to actuate a new and intense education, in order to discover all the richness contained in the new liturgy. Indeed, the liturgical renewal that has taken place since the Second Vatican Council has given, so to speak, greater visibility to the Eucharistic sacrifice. One factor contributing to this is that the words of the Eucharistic Prayer are said aloud by the celebrant, particularly the words of consecration, with the acclamation by the assembly immediately after the elevation.

All this should fill us with joy, but we should also remember that these changes demand new spiritual awareness and maturity, both on the part of the celebrant—especially now that he celebrates "facing the people"—and by the faithful. Eucharistic worship matures and grows when the words of the Eucharistic Prayer, especially the words of consecration, are spoken with great humility and simplicity, in a worthy and fitting way, which is understandable and in keeping with their holiness, when this essential act of the Eucharistic liturgy is performed unhurriedly, and when it brings about in us such recollection and devotion that the participants become aware of the greatness of the mystery being accomplished and show it by their attitude.

III. The Two Tables of the Lord and the Common Possession of the Church

The Table of the Word of God

10. We are well aware that from the earliest times the celebration of the Eucharist has been linked not only with prayer but also with the reading of Sacred Scripture and with singing by the whole assembly. As a result, it has long been possible to apply to the Mass the comparison, made by the Fathers, with the two tables, at which the Church prepares for her children the word of God and the Eucharist, that is, the bread of the Lord. We must therefore go back to the first part of the sacred mystery, the part that at present is most often called the liturgy of the Word, and devote some attention to it.

The reading of the passages of Sacred Scripture chosen for each day has been subjected by the Council to new criteria and requirements.[54] As a result of these norms of the Council a new collection of readings has been made, in which there has been applied to some extent the principle of continuity of texts and the principle of making all the sacred books accessible. The insertion of the psalms with responses into the liturgy makes the participants familiar with the great wealth of Old Testament prayer and poetry. The fact that these texts are read and sung in the vernacular enables everyone to participate with fuller understanding.

Nevertheless, there are also those people who, having been educated on the basis of the old liturgy in Latin, experience the lack of this "one language," which in all the world was an expression of the unity of the Church and through its dignified character elicited a profound sense of the Eucharistic mystery. It is therefore necessary to show not only understanding but also full respect toward these sentiments and desires. As far as possible these sentiments and desires are to be accommodated, as is moreover provided for in the new dispositions.[55] The Roman Church has special obligations toward Latin, the splendid language of ancient Rome, and she must manifest them whenever the occasion presents itself.

The possibilities that the post-conciliar renewal has introduced in this respect are indeed often utilized so as to make us witnesses of and sharers in the authentic celebration of the Word of God. There is also an increase in the number of people taking an active part in this celebration. Groups of readers and cantors, and still more often choirs of men or women, are being set up and are devoting themselves with great enthusiasm to this aspect. The Word of God, Sacred Scripture, is beginning to take on new life in many Christian communities. The faithful gathered for the liturgy prepare with song for listening to the Gospel, which is proclaimed with the devotion and love due to it.

All this is noted with great esteem and gratitude, but it must not be forgotten that complete renewal makes yet other demands. These demands consist in a new sense of responsibility toward the Word of God transmitted through the liturgy in various languages, something that is certainly in keeping with the universality of the Gospel and its purposes. The same sense of responsibility also involves the performance of the corresponding liturgical actions (reading or singing), which must accord with the principles of art. To preserve these actions from all artificiality, they should express such capacity, simplicity and dignity as to highlight the special character of the sacred text, even by the very manner of reading or singing.

Accordingly, these demands, which spring from a new responsibility for the Word of God in the liturgy,[56] go yet deeper and concern the inner attitude with which the ministers of the word perform their function in the liturgical assembly.[57] This responsibility also concerns the choice of texts. The choice has already been made by the competent ecclesiastical authority, which has also made provision for the cases in which readings more suited to a particular situation may be chosen.[58] Furthermore, it must always be remembered that only the Word of God can be used for Mass readings. The reading of Scripture cannot be replaced by the reading of other texts, however much they may be endowed with undoubted religious and moral values. On the other hand such texts can be used very profitably in the homily. Indeed the homily is supremely suitable for the use of such texts, provided that their content corresponds to the required conditions, since it is one of the tasks that belong to the nature of the homily to show the points of convergence between revealed divine wisdom and noble human thought seeking the truth by various paths.

The Table of the Bread of the Lord

11. The other table of the Eucharistic mystery, that of the bread of the Lord, also requires reflection from the viewpoint of the present-day liturgical renewal. This is a question of the greatest importance, since it concerns a special act of living faith, and indeed, as has been attested since the earliest centuries,[59] it is a manifestation of worship of Christ, who in Eucharistic Communion entrusts himself to each one of us, to our hearts, our consciences, our lips and our mouths in the form of food. Therefore there is special need, with regard to this question, for the watchfulness spoken of by the Gospel, on the part of the pastors who have charge of Eucharistic worship and on the part of the people of God, whose "sense of the faith"[60] must be very alert and acute particularly in this area.

I therefore wish to entrust this question to the heart of each one of you, venerable and dear brothers in the episcopate. You must above all make it part of your care for all the churches entrusted to you. I ask this of you in the name of the unity that we have received from the apostles as our heritage—collegial unity. This unity came to birth, in a sense, at the table of the bread of the Lord on Holy Thursday. With the help of your brothers in the priesthood, do all you can to safeguard the sacred dignity of the Eucharistic ministry and that deep spirit of Eucharistic Communion which belongs in a special way to the Church as the people of God, and which is also a particular heritage transmitted to us from the apostles, by various liturgical traditions, and by unnumbered generations of the faithful, who were often heroic witnesses to Christ, educated in "the school of the cross" (redemption) and of the Eucharist.

It must be remembered that the Eucharist as the table of the bread of the Lord is a continuous invitation. This is shown in the liturgy when the celebrant says: "This is the Lamb of God. Happy are those who are called to his supper."[61] It is also shown by the familiar Gospel parable about the guests invited to the marriage banquet.[62]

Let us remember that in this parable there are many who excuse themselves from accepting the invitation for various reasons.

Moreover our Catholic communities certainly do not lack people who could participate in Eucharistic Communion and do not, even though they have no serious sin on their conscience as an obstacle. To tell the truth, this attitude, which in some people is linked with an exaggerated severity, has changed in the present century, though it is still to be found here and there. In fact what one finds most often is not so much a feeling of unworthiness as a certain lack of interior willingness, if one may use this expression, a lack of Eucharistic "hunger" and "thirst," which is also a sign of lack of adequate sensitivity toward the great sacrament of love and a lack of understanding of its nature.

However, we also find in recent years another phenomenon. Sometimes, indeed quite frequently, everybody participating in the Eucharistic assembly goes to Communion, and on some such occasions, as experienced pastors confirm, there has not been due care to approach the sacrament of penance so as to purify one's conscience. This can of course mean that those approaching the Lord's table find nothing on their conscience, according to the objective law of God, to keep them from this sublime and joyful act of being sacramentally united with Christ. But there can also be, at least at times, another idea behind this: the idea of the Mass as only a banquet[63] in which one shares by receiving the body of Christ in order to manifest, above all else, fraternal communion. It is not hard to add to these reasons a certain human respect and mere "conformity."

This phenomenon demands from us watchful attention and a theological and pastoral analysis guided by a sense of great responsibility. We cannot allow the life of our communities to lose the good quality of sensitiveness of Christian conscience, guided solely by respect for Christ, who, when he is received in the Eucharist, should find in the heart of each of us a worthy abode. This question is closely linked not only with the practice of the sacrament of penance but also with a correct sense of responsibility for the whole deposit of moral teaching and for the precise distinction between good and evil, a distinction which then becomes for each person sharing in the Eucharist the basis for a correct judgment of self to be made in the depths of the personal conscience. St. Paul's words, "Let a man examine himself,"[64] are well known; this judgment is an indispensable condition for a personal decision whether to approach Eucharistic Communion or to abstain.

Celebration of the Eucharist places before us many other requirements regarding the ministry of the Eucharistic table. Some of these requirements concern only priests and deacons; others concern all who participate in the Eucharistic liturgy. Priests and deacons must remember that the service of the table of the bread of the Lord imposes on them special obligations which refer in the first place to Christ himself present in the Eucharist and second to all who actually participate in the Eucharist or who might do so. With regard to the first, perhaps it will not be superfluous to recall the words of the *Pontificale* which on the day of ordination the bishop addresses to the new priest as he hands to him on the paten and in the chalice the bread and wine offered by the faithful and prepared by the deacon: *"Accipe oblationem plebis sanctae Deo offerendam. Agnosce quod agis, imitare quod tractabis, et vitam tuam mysterio dominicae crucis conforma"*[65] ("Accept from the holy people of God the gifts to be offered to him. Know what you are doing, and imitate the mystery you celebrate: model your life on the mystery of the Lord's cross"). This last admonition made to him by the bishop should remain as one of the most precious norms of his Eucharistic ministry.

It is from this admonition that the priest's attitude in handling the bread and wine which have become the body and blood of the Redeemer should draw its inspiration. Thus it is necessary for all of us who are ministers of the Eucharist to examine carefully our actions at the altar, in particular the way in which we handle that food and drink which are the body and blood of the Lord our God in our hands, the way in which we distribute Holy Communion, and the way in which we perform the purification.

All these actions have a meaning of their own. Naturally, scrupulosity must be avoided, but God preserve us from behaving in a way that lacks respect, from undue hurry, from an impatience that causes scandal. Over and above our commitment to the evangelical mission, our greatest commitment consists in exercising this mysterious power over the body of the Redeemer, and all that is within us should be decisively ordered to this. We should also always remember that to this ministerial power we have been sacramentally consecrated, that we have been chosen from among men "for the good of men."[66] We especially, the priests of the Latin Church, whose ordination rite added in the course of the centuries the custom of anointing the priest's hands, should think about this.

In some countries the practice of receiving Communion in the hand has been introduced. This practice has been requested by individual episcopal conferences and has received approval from the Apostolic See. However, cases of a deplorable lack of respect toward the Eucharistic species have been reported, cases which are imputable not only to the individuals guilty of such behavior but also to the pastors of the church who have not been vigilant enough regarding the attitude of the faithful toward the Eucharist. It also happens, on occasion, that the free choice of those who prefer to continue the practice of receiving the Eucharist on the tongue is not taken into account in those places where the distribution of Communion in the hand has been authorized. It is therefore difficult in the context of this present letter not to mention the sad phenomena previously referred to. This is in no way meant to refer to those who, receiving the Lord Jesus in the hand, do so with profound reverence and devotion, in those countries where this practice has been authorized.

But one must not forget the primary office of priests who have been consecrated by their ordination to represent Christ the Priest. For this reason their hands, like their words and their will, have become the direct instruments of Christ. Through this fact, that is, as ministers of the Holy Eucharist, they have a primary responsibility for the sacred species, because it is a total responsibility. They offer the bread and wine, they consecrate it, and then they distribute the sacred species to the participants in the assembly who wish to receive them. Deacons can only bring to the altar the offerings of the faithful and, once they have been consecrated by the priest, distribute them. How eloquent therefore, even if not of ancient custom, is the rite of the anointing of the hands in our Latin ordination, as though precisely for these hands a special grace and power of the Holy Spirit is necessary!

To touch the sacred species and to distribute them with their own hands is a privilege of the ordained, one which indicates an active participation in the ministry of the Eucharist. It is obvious that the Church can grant this faculty to those who are neither priests nor deacons, as is the case with acolytes in the exercise of their ministry, especially if they are destined for future ordination, or with other lay people who are chosen for this to meet a just need, but always after an adequate preparation.

A Common Possession of the Church

12. We cannot, even for a moment, forget that the Eucharist is a special possession belonging to the whole Church. It is the greatest gift in the order of grace and of sacrament that the Divine Spouse has offered and unceasingly offers to his spouse. And precisely because it is such a gift, all of us should in a spirit of profound faith let ourselves be guided by a sense of truly Christian responsibility. A gift obliges us ever more profoundly because it speaks to us not so much with the force of a strict right as with the force of personal confidence, and thus—without legal obligations—it calls for trust and gratitude. The Eucharist is just such a gift and such a possession. We should remain faithful in every detail to what it expresses in itself and to what it asks of us, namely thanksgiving.

The Eucharist is a common possession of the whole Church as the sacrament of her unity. And thus the Church has the strict duty to specify everything which concerns participation in it and its celebration. We should therefore act according to the principles laid down by the last Council, which, in the *Constitution on the Sacred Liturgy,* defined the authorizations and obligations of individual bishops in their dioceses and of the episcopal conferences, given the fact that both act in collegial unity with the Apostolic See.

Furthermore we should follow the directives issued by the various departments of the Holy See in this field, be it in liturgical matters, in the rules established by the liturgical books in what concerns the Eucharistic mystery, and in the instructions devoted to this mystery,[67] be it with regard to *communicatio in sacris,* in the norms of the Ecumenical Directory[68] and in the Instruction Concerning Particular Cases When Other Christians May Be Admitted to Eucharistic Communion in the Catholic Church.[69] And although at this stage of renewal the possibility of a certain "creative" freedom has been permitted, nevertheless this freedom must strictly respect the requirements of substantial unity. We can follow the path of this pluralism (which arises in part from the introduction itself of the various languages into the liturgy) only as long as the essential characteristics of the celebration of the Eucharist are preserved and the norms prescribed by the recent liturgical reform are respected.

Indispensable effort is required everywhere to ensure that within the pluralism of Eucharistic worship envisioned by the Second Vatican Council the unity of which the Eucharist is the sign and cause is clearly manifested.

This task, over which in the nature of things the Apostolic See must keep careful watch, should be assumed not only by each episcopal conference but by every minister of the Eucharist, without exception. Each one should also remember that he is responsible for the common good of the whole Church. The priest as minister, as celebrant, as the one who presides over the Eucharistic assembly of the faithful, should have a special sense of the common good of the Church, which he represents through his ministry, but to which he must also be subordinate, according to a correct discipline of faith. He cannot consider himself a "proprietor" who can make free use of the liturgical text and of the sacred rite as if it were his own property, in such a way as to stamp it with his own arbitrary personal style. At times this latter might seem more effective, and it may better correspond to subjective piety; nevertheless, objectively it is always a betrayal of that union which should find its proper expression in the sacrament of unity.

Every priest who offers the holy sacrifice should recall that during this sacrifice it is not only he with his community that is praying but the whole Church, which is thus expressing in this sacrament her spiritual unity, among other ways by the use of the approved liturgical text. To call this position "mere insistence on uniformity" would only show ignorance of the objective requirements of authentic unity and would be a symptom of harmful individualism.

This subordination of the minister, of the celebrant, to the *mysterium* which has been entrusted to him by the Church for the good of the whole people of God should also find expression in the observance of the liturgical requirements concerning the celebration of the holy sacrifice. These refer for example to dress, and in particular to the vestments worn by the celebrant. Circumstances have of course existed and continue to exist in which the prescriptions do not oblige. We have been greatly moved when reading books, written by priests who had been prisoners in extermination camps, with descriptions of Eucharistic celebrations without the above-mentioned rules, that is to say, without an altar and without vestments. But although in those conditions this was a proof of heroism and deserved profound admiration, nevertheless in normal conditions to ignore the liturgical directives can be interpreted as a lack of respect toward the Eucharist, dictated perhaps by individualism or by an absence of a critical sense concerning current opinions, or by a certain lack of a spirit of faith.

Upon all of us who, through the grace of God, are ministers of the Eucharist there weighs a particular responsibility for the ideas and attitudes of our brothers and sisters who have been entrusted to our pastoral care. It is our vocation to nurture, above all by personal example, every healthy manifestation of worship toward Christ present and operative in that sacrament of love. May God preserve us from acting otherwise and weakening that worship by "becoming unaccustomed" to various manifestations and forms of Eucharistic worship which express a perhaps "traditional" but healthy piety, and which express above all that "sense of the faith" possessed by the whole people of God, as the Second Vatican Council recalled.[70]

As I bring these considerations to an end, I would like to ask forgiveness—in my own name and in the name of all of you, venerable and dear brothers in the episcopate—for everything which, for whatever reason, through whatever human weakness, impatience or negligence, and also through the at times partial, one-sided and erroneous application of the directives of the Second Vatican Council, may have caused scandal and disturbance concerning the interpretation of the doctrine and the veneration due to this great sacrament. And I pray the Lord Jesus that in the future we may avoid in our manner of dealing with this sacred mystery anything that could weaken or disorient in any way the sense of reverence and love that exists in our faithful people.

May Christ himself help us to follow the path of true renewal toward that fullness of life and of Eucharistic worship whereby the

Church is built up in that unity that she already possesses, and which she desires to bring to ever greater perfection for the glory of the living God and for the salvation of all humanity.

Conclusion

13. Permit me, venerable and dear brothers, to end these reflections of mine, which have been restricted to a detailed examination of only a few questions. In undertaking these reflections, I have had before my eyes all the work carried out by the Second Vatican Council, and have kept in mind Paul VI's encyclical *Mysterium Fidei* promulgated during that Council and all the documents issued after the same Council for the purpose of implementing the post-conciliar liturgical renewal. A very close and organic bond exists between the renewal of the liturgy and the renewal of the whole life of the Church.

The Church not only acts but also expresses herself in the liturgy, lives by the liturgy and draws from the liturgy the strength of her life. For this reason liturgical renewal carried out correctly in the spirit of the Second Vatican Council is, in a certain sense, the measure and the condition for putting into effect the teaching of that Council which we wish to accept with profound faith, convinced as we are that by means of this Council the Holy Spirit "has spoken to the Church" the truths and given the indications for carrying out her mission among the people of today and tomorrow.

We shall continue in the future to take special care to promote and follow the renewal of the Church according to the teaching of the Second Vatican Council, in the spirit of an ever living tradition. In fact to the substance of tradition properly understood belongs also a correct rereading of the "signs of the times," which require us to draw from the rich treasure of revelation "things both new and old."[71] Acting in this spirit, in accordance with this counsel of the Gospel, the Second Vatican Council carried out a providential effort to renew the face of the Church in the sacred liturgy, most often having recourse to what is "ancient," what comes from the heritage of the Fathers and is the expression of the faith and doctrine of a Church that has remained united for so many centuries.

In order to be able to continue in the future to put into practice the directives of the Council in the field of liturgy, and in particular in the field of Eucharistic worship, close collaboration is necessary between the competent department of the Holy See and each episcopal conference, a collaboration that must be at the same time vigilant and creative. We must keep our sights fixed on the greatness of the most holy mystery and at the same time on spiritual movements and social changes which are so significant for our times, since they not only sometimes create difficulties but also prepare us for a new way of participating in that great mystery of faith.

Above all I wish to emphasize that the problems of the liturgy, and in particular of the Eucharistic liturgy, must not be an occasion for dividing Catholics and for threatening the unity of the Church. This is demanded by an elementary understanding of that sacrament which Christ has left us as the source of spiritual unity. And how could the Eucharist, which in the Church is the *sacramentum pietatis, signum unitatis, vinculum caritatis* (sacrament of piety, sign of unity, bond of love),[72] form between us at this time a point of division and a source of distortion of thought and of behavior, instead of being the focal point and constitutive center, which it truly is in its essence, of the unity of the Church herself?

We are all equally indebted to our Redeemer. We should all listen together to that Spirit of truth and of love whom he has promised to the Church and who is operative in her. In the name of this truth and of this love, in the name of the crucified Christ and of his mother, I ask you, and beg you: Let us abandon all opposition and division, and let us all unite in this great mission of salvation which is the price and at the same time the fruit of our redemption. The Apostolic See will continue to do all that is possible to provide the means of ensuring that unity of which we speak. Let everyone avoid anything in his own way of acting which could "grieve the Holy Spirit."[73]

In order that this unity and the constant and systematic collaboration which leads to it may be perseveringly continued, I beg on my knees that, through the intercession of Mary, holy spouse of the Holy Spirit and mother of the Church, we may all receive the light of the Holy Spirit. And blessing everyone, with all my heart I once more address myself to you, my venerable and dear brothers in the episcopate, with a fraternal greeting and with full trust. In this collegial unity in which we share, let us do all we can to ensure that the Eucharist may become an ever greater source of life and light for the consciences of all our brothers and sisters of all the communities in the universal unity of Christ's Church on earth.

In a spirit of fraternal charity, to you and to all our confreres in the priesthood I cordially impart the apostolic blessing.

From the Vatican, February 24, First Sunday of Lent, in the year 1980, the second of our pontificate.

Pope John Paul II

Notes

1. Cf. Chapter 2: AAS 71 (1979), pp. 395f.

2. Cf. Ecumenical Council of Trent, Session XXII, Can. 2: *Conciliorum Oecumenicorum Decreta,* ed. 3, Bologna 1973, p. 735.

3. Because of this precept of the Lord, an Ethiopian Eucharistic liturgy recalls that the apostles "established for us patriarchs, archbishops, priests and deacons to celebrate the ritual of your holy Church": *Anaphora Sancti Athanasii: Prex Eucharistica,* Haenggi-Pahl, Fribourg (Switzerland) 1968, p. 183.

4. Cf. *La Tradition apostolique de saint Hippolyte,* nos. 2–4, ed. Botte, Münster-Westfalen 1963, pp. 5–17.

5. 2 Cor. 11:28.

6. 1 Pt. 2:5.

7. Cf. Second Vatican Ecumenical Council, Dogmatic Constitution on the Church *Lumen Gentium,* 28; AAS 57 (1965), pp. 33f; Decree on the Ministry and Life of Priests *Presbyterorum Ordinis,* 2, 5: AAS 58 (1966), pp. 993, 998; Decree on the Missionary Activity of the Church *Ad Gentes,* 39: AAS 58 (1966), p. 986.

8. Second Vatican Ecumenical Council, Dogmatic Constitution on the Church 11: AAS 57 (1965), p. 15.

9. Jn. 3:16. It is interesting to note how these words are taken up by the liturgy of St. John Chrysostom immediately before the words of consecration and introduce the latter: cf. *La divina Liturgia del nostro Padre Giovanni Crisostomo,* Roma-Grottaferrata 1967, pp. 104f.

10. Cf. Mt. 26:26–28; Mk. 14:22–25; Lk. 22:18–20; 1 Cor. 11:23–25; cf. also the Eucharistic Prayers.

11. Phil. 2:8.

12. Jn. 13:1.

13. Cf. John Paul II, Homily in Phoenix Park, Dublin, 7: AAS 71 (1979), pp. 1074ff; Sacred Congregation of Rites, instruction *Eucharisticum Mysterium:* AAS 59 (1967), pp. 539–573; Roman Ritual, "Holy Communion and Worship of the Eucharist Outside of Mass," ed. typica, 1973. It should be noted that the value of the worship and the sanctifying power of these forms of devotion to the Eucharist depend not so much upon the forms themselves as upon interior attitudes.

14. Cf. Bull *Transiturus de hoc mundo* (Aug. 11, 1264): Aemilii Friedberg, *Corpus Iuris Canonici,* Pars II. *Decretalium Collectiones,* Leipzig 1881, pp. 1174–1177; *Studi eucaristici, VII Centenario della Bolla 'Transiturus' 1264–1964,* Orvieto 1966, pp. 302–317.

15. Cf. Paul VI, encyclical letter *Mysterium Fidei:* AAS 57 (1965), pp. 753–774; Sacred Congregation of Rites, instruction *Eucharisticum Mysterium:* AAS 59 (1967), pp. 539–573; Roman Ritual, "Holy Communion and Worship of the Eucharist Outside of Mass," ed. typica, 1973.

16. John Paul II, encyclical letter *Redemptor Hominis,* 20: AAS 71 (1979), p. 311; cf. Second Vatican Ecumenical Council, Dogmatic Constitution on the Church, 11: AAS 57 (1965), pp. 15f; also, note 57 to Schema II of the same dogmatic constitution, in *Acta Synodalia Sacrosancti Concilii Oecumenici Vaticani II,* vol. II, periodus 2a, pars I, public session II, pp. 251f; Paul VI, Address at the General Audience of Sept. 15, 1965: *Insegnamenti di Paolo VI,* III (1965), p. 1036; H. de Lubac, *Meditation sur l'Eglise,* 2 ed., Paris 1963, pp. 129–137.

17. 1 Cor. 11:26.

18. Cf. Second Vatican Ecumenical Council, Dogmatic Constitution on the Church, 11: AAS 57 (1965) pp. 15f; Constitution on the Sacred Liturgy *Sacrosanctum Concilium,* 10: AAS 56 (1964), p. 102; Decree on the Ministry and Life of Priests, 5: AAS 58 (1966), pp. 997f; Decree on the Bishops' Pastoral Office in the Church *Christus Dominus,* 30: AAS 58 (1966), pp. 668f; Decree on the Church's Missionary Activity, 9: AAS 58(1966), pp. 957f.

19. Cf. Second Vatican Ecumenical Council, Dogmatic Constitution on the Church, 26: AAS 57 (1965), pp. 31f; Decree on Ecumenism *Unitatis Redintegratio,* 15: AAS 57 (1965), pp. 101f.

20. This is what the Opening Prayer of Holy Thursday asks for: "We pray that in this Eucharist we may find the fullness of love and life": Roman Missal, ed. typica altera 1975, p. 244; also the Communion epiclesis of the Roman Missal: "May all of us who share in the body and blood of Christ be brought together in unity by the Holy Spirit. Lord, remember your Church throughout the world; make us grow in love": Eucharistic Prayer II: *ibid.,* pp. 458f; Eucharistic Prayer III, p. 463.

21. Jn. 5:17.

22. Cf. Prayer after Communion of the Mass for the 22nd Sunday in Ordinary Time: "Lord, you renew us at your table with the bread of life. May this food strengthen us in love and help us to serve you in each other": Roman Missal, ed. cit., p. 361.

23. Jn. 4:23.

24. Cf. 1 Cor. 10:17; commented upon by St. Augustine: *In Evangelium Ioannis tract.* 31, 13; PL 35, 1613; also commented upon by the Ecumenical Council of Trent, Session XIII, can. 8; *Conciliorum Oecumenicorum Decreta,* ed. 3, Bologna 1973, p. 697, 7; cf. Second Vatican Ecumenical Council, Dogmatic Constitution on the Church, 7: AAS 57 (1965), p. 9.

25. Jn. 13:35.

26. This is expressed by many prayers of the Roman Missal: the Prayer over the Gifts from the Common, "For those who work for the underprivileged"; "May we who celebrate the love of your Son also follow the example of your saints and grow in love for you and for one another"; Roman Missal, ed. cit., p. 721; also the Prayer after Communion of the Mass "For Teachers": "May this holy meal help us to follow the example of your saints by showing in our lives the light of truth and love for our brothers"; *ibid.,* p. 723; cf. also the Prayer after Communion of the Mass for the 22nd Sunday in ordinary time, quoted in note 22.

27. Jn. 4:23.

28. Eph. 4:13.

29. Cf. above, no. 2.

30. Cf. Second Vatican Ecumenical Council, Decree on the Missionary Activity of the Church, 9, 13: AAS 58 (1966), pp. 958, 961f; Decree on the Ministry and Life of Priests, 5: AAS 58 (1966), p. 997.

31. 1 Jn. 3:1.

32. Second Vatican Ecumenical Council, Dogmatic Constitution on the Church, 11: AAS 57 (1965), p. 15.

33. Cf. no. 20: AAS 71 (1979), pp. 313f.

34. 2 Pt. 3:13.

35. Col. 3:10.

36. Lk. 1:34; Jn. 6:69; Acts 3:14; Rev. 3:7.

37. Acts 10:38; Lk. 4:18.

38. Jn. 10:36.

39. Cf. Jn. 10:17.

40. Heb. 3:1; 4:15, etc.

41. As was stated in the ninth century Byzantine liturgy, according to the most ancient codex, known formerly as *Barberino di San Marco* (Florence), and, now that it is kept in the Vatican Apostolic Library, as *Barberini*

Greco 366 fo. 8 verso, lines 17–20. This part has been published by F. E. Brightman, *Liturgies Eastern and Western,* I. *Eastern Liturgies,* Oxford 1896, p. 318, 34–35.

42. Opening Prayer of the Second Votive Mass of the Holy Eucharist: Roman Missal, ed. cit., p. 858.

43. 1 Jn. 2:2; cf. *ibid.,* 4:10.

44. We speak of the *Divinum Mysterium,* the *Sanctissimum,* the *Sacrosanctum,* meaning what is sacred and holy par excellence. For their part, the Eastern churches call the Mass *raza* or *mysterion, hagiasmos, quddasa, qedasse,* that is to say "consecration" par excellence. Furthermore there are the liturgical rites, which, in order to inspire a sense of the sacred, prescribe silence, and standing or kneeling, and likewise professions of faith, and the incensation of the Book of the Gospels, the altar, the celebrant and the sacred species. They even recall the assistance of the angelic beings created to serve the Holy God, i.e., with the *Sanctus* of our Latin churches and the *Trisagion* and *Sancta Sanctis* of the Eastern liturgies.

45. For instance, in the invitation to receive Communion, this faith has been so formed as to reveal complementary aspects of the presence of Christ the Holy One: the epiphanic aspect noted by the Byzantines ("Blessed is he who comes in the name of the Lord: The Lord is God and *has appeared to us": La divina Liturgia del santo nostro Padre Giovanni Crisostomo,* Roma-Grottaferrata 1967 pp. 136f); the aspect of relation and union sung of by the Armenians (Liturgy of St. Ignatius of Antioch: *"Unus Pater sanctus nobiscum, unus Filius sanctus nobiscum, unus Spiritus sanctus nobiscum":* Die Anaphora des heiligen Ignatius von Antiochien, ubersetzt von A. Rucker, *Oriens Christianus,* 3a ser., 5 (1930), p. 76); and the hidden heavenly aspect celebrated by the Chaldeans and Malabars (cf. the antiphonal hymn sung by the priest and the assembly after Communion: F. E. Brightman, op. cit., p. 299).

46. Cf. Second Vatican Ecumenical Council, Constitution on the Sacred Liturgy, 2, 47: AAS 56 (1964), pp. 83f; 113; Dogmatic Constitution on the Church, 3 and 28: AAS 57 (1965) , pp. 6, 33f; Decree on Ecumenism, 2: AAS 57 (1965), p. 91: Decree on the Ministry and Life of Priests, 13: AAS 58 (1966), pp. 1011f; Ecumenical Council of Trent, Session XXII, chap. I and II: *Conciliorum Oecumenicorum Decreta,* ed. 3, Bologna 1973, pp. 732f; especially: *una eademque est hostia, idem nunc offerens sacerdotum ministerio, qui se ipsum tunc in cruce obtulit, sola offerendi ratione diversa (ibid.,* p. 733).

47. Synodus Constantinopolita adversus Sotericum (January 1156 and May 1157): Angelo Mai, *Spicilegium romanum,* t. X, Rome 1844, p. 77; PG

140, 190; cf. Martin Jugie, *Dict. Theol. Cath.,* t. X, 1338; *Theologia dogmatica christianorum orientalium,* Paris 1930, pp. 317–320.

48. General Instruction of the Roman Missal, 49c: Roman Missal, ed. cit., p. 39; cf. Second Vatican Ecumenical Council, Decree on the Ministry and Life of Priests, 5: AAS 58 (1966), pp. 997f.

49. The Rite of Mass With a Congregation, 18: Roman Missal, ed. cit. p. 390.

50. Cf. Ecumenical Council of Trent, Session 22, chap. 1, *Conciliorum Oecumenicorum Decreta,* ed. 3, Bologna 1973, pp. 732f.

51. Col. 2:14.

52. Jn. 11:28.

53. General Instruction of the Roman Missal, 55f.: Roman Missal, ed. cit., p. 40.

54. Cf. Constitution on the Sacred Liturgy, 35, 51: AAS 56 (1964), pp. 109, 114.

55. Cf. Sacred Congregation of Rites, Instruction on the Language to Be Used in the Liturgy of the Hours and the Eucharist, VI, 17–18; VII, 19–20: AAS 57 (1965), pp. 1012f; Instruction on Sacred Music, IV, 48: AAS 59 (1967), p. 314; Decree on the Titles of Minor Basilicas, II, 8: AAS 60 (1968), p. 538; Sacred Congregation for Divine Worship, Notification: The Roman Missal, Liturgy of the Hours, Calendar, I, 4: AAS 63 (1971), p. 714.

56. Cf. Paul VI, apostolic constitution *Missale Romanum:* "We are fully confident that both priests and faithful will prepare their minds and hearts more devoutly for the Lord's Supper, meditating on the Scriptures, nourished day by day with the words of the Lord": AAS 61 (1969), pp. 220f.; Roman Missal, ed. cit., p. 15.

57. Cf. Roman Pontifical. The Institution of Lector and Acolytes, 4, ed. typica, 1972, pp. 19f.

58. Cf. General Instruction of the Roman Missal, 319–320: Roman Missal, ed. cit., p. 87.

59. Cf. Fr. J. Dolger, *Das Segnen der Sinne mit der Eucharistie. Eine altchristliche Kommunionsitte: Antike und Christentum,* t. 3 (1932), pp. 231–244; *Das Kultvergehen der Donatistin Lucilla von Karthago. Reliquienkuss vor dem Kuss der Eucharistie, ibid.,* pp. 245–252.

60. Cf. Second Vatican Ecumenical Council, Dogmatic Constitution on the Church, 12, 35; AAS 57 (1965), pp. 16, 40.

61. Cf. Jn. 1:29; Rv. 19:9.

62. Cf. Lk. 14:16ff.

63. Cf. General Instruction of the Roman Missal, 7–8: Roman Missal, ed. cit., p. 29.

64. 1 Cor. 11:28.

65. Roman Pontifical. The Ordination of Deacons, Priests and Bishops, ed. typica, 1968, p. 93.

66. Heb. 5:1.

67. Sacred Congregation of Rites, Instruction on Eucharistic Worship: AAS 59 (1967), pp. 539–573; Roman Ritual. Holy Communion and Worship of the Eucharist Outside of Mass, ed. typica, 1973; Sacred Congregation for Divine Worship, Circular Letter to Presidents of Episcopal Conferences on Eucharistic Prayers: AAS 65 (1973), pp. 340–347.

68. Nos. 38–63: AAS 59 (1967), pp. 586–592.

69. AAS 64 (1972), pp. 518–525. Cf. also the *Communicatio* published the following year for the correct application of the above-mentioned instruction: AAS 65 (1973), pp. 616–619.

70. Cf. Second Vatican Ecumenical Council, Dogmatic Constitution on the Church, 12: AAS 57 (1965), pp. 16f.

71. Mt. 13:52.

72. Cf. St. Augustine, *In Evangelium Ioannis tract.* 26, 13: PL 35, 1612f.

73. Eph. 4:30.